Vintage MIAMI BEACH GLAMOUR

CELEBRITIES & SOCIALITES IN THE HEYDAY OF CHIC

DEBORAH C. POLLACK

*Foreword by Paul S. George, PhD
Resident Historian, HistoryMiami Museum*

Published by The History Press
Charleston, SC
www.historypress.com

Copyright © 2019 by Deborah C. Pollack
All rights reserved

Front cover, left: Elizabeth Taylor and William "Bill" Pawley Jr., June 8, 1949, Miami Beach. *MBVCA Collection, HistoryMiami, P109A*; *center*: Tennis champion Marta Barnett posing in Miami Beach, 1939. *State Archives of Florida*; *right*: Candid photograph of Linda Darnell, Richard Widmark and Veronica Lake relaxing on the set of *Slattery's Hurricane* at Villa Tranquilla, Miami Beach, 1948. *Miami News Collection, HistoryMiami Museum, 1989-011-21820*, *bottom*: Burdine's Sunshine Fashions show at the Roney Plaza, Miami Beach, February 3, 1933. *Acme Newspictures, author's collection.*
Back cover, top: Aerial view of the Nautilus Hotel, 1936. *Albertype postcard, State Archives of Florida*; *bottom*: Winston Churchill painting in Frank Clarke's cabana at the Surf Club, 1946. *State Archives of Florida.*

First published 2019

Manufactured in the United States

ISBN 9781467141581

Library of Congress Control Number: 2018958986

Notice: The information in this book is true and complete to the best of our knowledge. It is offered without guarantee on the part of the author or The History Press. The author and The History Press disclaim all liability in connection with the use of this book.

All rights reserved. No part of this book may be reproduced or transmitted in any form whatsoever without prior written permission from the publisher except in the case of brief quotations embodied in critical articles and reviews.

CONTENTS

Foreword, by Paul S. George, PhD   5
Acknowledgements   7
Introduction   9

1. Introducing Count George du Manoir and
    His Miami Beach   13
2. The Fashionable Life at Private Clubs, Hotels and Parties   20
3. The Sporting Life in and around Miami Beach   39
4. Miami Beach Personalities: The High-Flying du Ponts,
    Talented Firestones and the Remarkable Shirley Cowell   47
5. A New Versailles and a Second World War   55
6. The Count's Friend Hosts the Winston Churchills   59
7. Hialeah Memories   65
8. Hollywood Comes to Miami Beach   73
9. "Blimping Along Over Miami Beach"   83
10. Intriguing Stories behind Miami Beach's
    Most Beautiful Faces   88
11. Nightclubbing with the Rich and Famous   108
12. Destinations of Miami Beach's Colony:
    "La Habana Cuba," Nassau and the Florida Keys   113
13. Miami Beach Culture for the Rich and Not So Rich   119
14. The Count's Friendships with Other
    Influential South Floridians   128

Contents

15. Miami Beach Holidays with Jane Fisher, "Suzy," the "Tango Queen" and an Ice Cream Soda	130
16. The Miami Beach Club Crowd during the Off-Season	138
17. Scandals Brush the Beach	141
18. A Farewell to the Count's Miami Beach	150
Notes	155
Bibliography	177
Index	183
About the Author	191

FOREWORD

Miami Beach assumed its place as a premier tourist resort in the 1920s, little more than five years after its incorporation, as Carl Fisher, its earliest, most important developer and promoter, had visualized. And its popularity grew as the years and decades unfolded, reaching a peak in the 1960s, when "the Beach" was arguably America's preeminent vacation spot, before entering a lengthy period of decline. The island's return to prominence was the result of an unforeseen development: the rise in popularity in the late 1980s and beyond of a blighted, aged neighborhood in South Beach that is today's world-famous Art Deco District.

From the 1920s into the 1960s, the Beach could claim at least two levels of tourists. The first was made up of those of the familiar postcard variety where visitors dotted its broad beaches, patronized its lively nightclubs and filled the rapidly growing canyon of hotels rising along Collins Avenue, tourism's Main Street and a thoroughfare unlike that of any other resort in the world. In those early postwar years, everyone seemingly had experienced the Beach or knew someone who had done so. Less known were members of America's and the Western world's "royalty," be they entrepreneurs of leading companies, heirs and heiresses with European titles and fortunes or famed figures from the worlds of entertainment, sports and politics. They composed another level of visitor. Their lair included the exclusive Bath and Surf clubs, as well as the lavish winter homes of American millionaires on the dredged islands of Biscayne Bay or along the exclusive streets whose names—LaGorce Drive, North Bay Road and Pinetree Drive—were redolent of exclusivity.

Foreword

Deborah C. Pollack, a gifted writer, art historian and art dealer, has provided readers with *Vintage Miami Beach Glamour: Celebrities and Socialites in the Heyday of Chic*, a penetrating look into the latter category of visitor/winter resident, through the voluminous writings of Count George Le Pelley du Manoir, a well-traveled favorite of the high society world of the Beach. Du Manoir was introduced to this rarified world by Robert and Evelyn Gifford, a wealthy couple who owned a large home in Miami Beach and who invited him to stay with them for the winter of 1931. The count quickly became a mainstay of that scene, befriending many among the rich and famous for the next three decades, while becoming its unofficial chronicler.

Pollack draws on the written insights of the urbane, charismatic French count to examine and explain the evolution of the famed resort through the activities and relationships, sometimes scandalous, often fraught, of its wealthiest, most entitled visitors, whose ranks ranged from Winston Churchill to Elizabeth Taylor. Heretofore, we knew of their presence primarily through society and gossip columns. But the count's written observations—some appearing in newsletters and magazines—bring their lives (and his) in the winter playground into sharp relief.

As Pollack has noted, du Manoir's address book often reads like "part *Social Register*, part *Who's Who of Miami Beach* and part *Who's Who in the World.*" Pollack skillfully weaves her narrative around these characters and places the story in a broad historical context reaching beyond Miami Beach to other enclaves of the wealthy and privileged. Further, the author's judicious employment of photographs, especially those of these reclusive visitors, embellishes her rich narrative.

That du Manoir could thrive for three decades in a milieu so different from his earlier life attests to his own resources, his work ethic and the love many of this royalty exhibited toward him. Ultimately, du Manoir and his cast of friends and acquaintances moved on from Miami Beach. The count relocated to Palm Beach, married a wealthy widow in 1963 and lived in that area until his death at age ninety-five in 1992. His departure, as well as those of many of his longtime friends, left Miami Beach bereft of an element of class and accomplishment. Subsequent years saw a sharp decline in the fortunes of the island until its reincarnation of recent years. Yet the presence of royalty as manifest in du Manoir and his peers in the middle decades of the twentieth century disappeared with their exodus.

Paul S. George, PhD,
Resident Historian, HistoryMiami Museum

ACKNOWLEDGEMENTS

I would first like to thank Amanda Irle, acquisitions editor of The History Press, for her enthusiasm and assistance. I am additionally grateful to Adam Ferrell, publishing director, and the entire staff and board of The History Press.

My gratitude also extends to my fabulous mom, P.J.; my wonderful husband, Ed; and the following people and institutions: Laurie Austin, AV archives, John F. Kennedy Presidential Library and Museum; Robert W. Avent; Kim Bedetti, Monmouth County Historical Association; Brooke Russell Astor Reading Room for Rare Books and Manuscripts, the New York Public Library; Paul S. George, PhD, resident historian, HistoryMiami Museum; Nick Golubov, research director, Historical Society of Palm Beach County; Maryrose Grossman, AV archives reference, John F. Kennedy Presidential Library and Museum; Nicola Hellmann-McFarland Sr., library assistant, special collections, University of Miami Libraries; Wendy S. Israel, deputy director, editorial operations, Hearst Magazines; Jeremy Johnson, president and CEO, Historical Society of Palm Beach County; Martha L. Kearsley; Kristen Lachterman, collections assistant, HistoryMiami Museum; Vance Lauderdale; Pamela Nash Mathews; Jim Mitchell; Debi Murray, chief curator, Historical Society of Palm Beach County; Linda Nardi, managing editor, *Town & Country*; Jessica Purkis, AV archives reference, John F. Kennedy Presidential Library and Museum; Jennifer J. Quan, intellectual property manager, John F. Kennedy Library Foundation; Annamaria Richcreek, administrator, Montgomery Botanical

Acknowledgements

Center; State Archives of Florida; Ashley Trujillo, archives manager, HistoryMiami Museum; Effie Westervelt; and Megan Woods, AV archives reference, John F. Kennedy Presidential Library and Museum.

INTRODUCTION

Once upon a time in Miami Beach, clothes were smart, blondes were anything but dumb, men were wolves, gay meant carefree and cocktail parties included seven hundred of one's most intimate friends. Indeed, everyone knew everyone else when one's only social networking tools were private clubs, a telephone, stationery and an address book.

This is a history of vintage, privileged Miami Beach and their milieu from roughly 1930 to 1960. The winter colony's glamorous and sometimes scandalous world extended across Biscayne Bay to Miami, Coral Gables and Hialeah Park; due north to neighboring Surfside and farther to Sunny Isles, Hallandale and Palm Beach; south to the Keys, east to Nassau and southeast to Havana. The elite clique led seemingly idyllic lives drenched in a golden glow of the sun by day and the famous Miami moon at night, but trouble and tragedy touched them, no matter how wealthy or beautiful.

They could each write a book on the art of fine living and mixed with Hollywood celebrities, including Elizabeth Taylor, and historic figures, such as Winston Churchill, as effortlessly as tonic mixes with gin. Nicknames were plentiful—Bunty, Nixie, Bab, Winnie, Woolie, Brownie, Budge and Titter—and every few years, ex-spouses were passed from one socialite to another like hors d'oeuvre. Exes co-hosted parties and danced with each other, and no matter how strong their grudges brewed behind their smiling faces, everyone stayed cordial so they could all have a delightful season.

The abundance of socializing; culture; tennis, golf and bridge tournaments; regattas; and horse racing enticed Palm Beach residents, who

Introduction

made the trip south by yacht, train, plane or chauffeur-driven automobile. In fact, the camaraderie between the two enclaves would never be as strong as it was during those vintage years. In the off-season, winter denizens of both places flew north to Washington, D.C.; Philadelphia; New York City; Southampton; Chicago; Europe; and beyond.

This historical account of the Miami Beach social circle is told in part through the eyes, ears and typewriter of a prominent person who lived it: Count George du Manoir. His address book, circa 1939, reads like a part *Social Register*, part *Who's Who of Miami Beach* and part *Who's Who in the World*. Along with members of nobility (including Count René Chambrun, the great-great-grandson of the Marquis de Lafayette and famed French attorney of Coco Chanel) and royalty (such as Prince Georges Alexandrovich Stroganoff Scherbatoff, a U.S. intelligence agent for Franklin Delano Roosevelt), du Manoir listed many other luminaries, most of them philanthropic: Bernard Baruch; Edsel Ford; William K. Vanderbilt II; Charles and Anne Morrow Lindbergh; founding donator to the National Gallery of Art and Hialeah Park Race Track owner Joseph E. Widener; Fairchild Tropical Botanic Garden founder Colonel Robert H. Montgomery; the garden's namesake, David Fairchild; the du Pont, Carnegie and Firestone families; Yellow Cab and rental car king John D. Hertz; Miami banking business mogul and nature lover Frank Smathers Jr.; the Fanjul family, sugar barons who would later emigrate from Cuba to Florida; internationally recognized artist Wheeler Williams; former governor of Ohio James Middleton Cox and his son, media magnate James McMahon Cox; Norman Bailey Woolworth from the dime store dynasty; Surf Club vice president and secretary Alfred I. Barton; Miami pioneer banker James Gilman, who, along with J.E. Lummus, helped to financially stabilize the city after the disastrous 1926 hurricane; movie theater pioneer and Sunset Islands developer Stephen Andrew Lynch; entertainer Kitty Carlisle; Gloria Morgan Vanderbilt; and British aircraft manufacturer Frederick Sigrist. Additional famous friends included environmentalist Marjory Stoneman Douglas; Carl Fisher's ex-wife, Jane Fisher; multimillionaire inventor and racer Garfield "Gar" Wood; celebrated writer Damon Runyon; Miami Beach pioneer and developer Thomas J. Pancoast; and playboy John Jacob Astor VI.

Du Manoir's exciting life intertwined with all these significant people, as well as other notables who impacted Miami Beach. He expressed his observations and thoughts in typewritten essays beginning in the 1930s, some perhaps printed in lost periodicals, but a few so outrageous they were likely unpublished. Revealing goings-on at private clubs and parties as well as

Introduction

historic events, his numerous articles from the late 1940s, likely for a private club newsletter, were as light and frothy as champagne bubbles, which is precisely what he titled most of them. The count's columns in manuscript form on browned, fragile paper were found in a three-ringed portfolio among his other archives. Fortunate enough to have discovered the treasure, the author presents this fascinating Miami Beach era to you.

Chapter 1
INTRODUCING COUNT GEORGE DU MANOIR AND HIS MIAMI BEACH

On October 14, 1925, a fit and attractive twenty-eight-year-old French viscount named Georges Henri Marie Le Pelley du Manoir disembarked from the SS *Paris* at New York City. Blessed with impeccable breeding, athletic ability, gumption, style and grace, he had everything a man could want—except an abundant amount of money. He Americanized his first name as "George" on the passenger list and gave his occupation as manufacturer, but his main product was charisma. After traveling briefly to Montreal, he returned to the United States as an immigrant, arriving on August 10, 1926, at Rouses Point in New York State, just south of the Canadian border.[1]

Born into French nobility on August 2, 1897, at Vaucresson, a suburb of Paris, Vicomte Georges Henri Marie Le Pelley du Manoir was a descendant of Pierre René Marie Dumanoir Le Pelley (1770–1829), as well as Jacques Romain Henri Armand Le Pelley Dumanoir. Another relative, Ferdinand Marie, Vicomte de Lesseps (1805–1894), was a renowned diplomat who developed the Suez Canal. Du Manoir's parents were Mathieu Jules Marie René, Vicomte Le Pelley du Manoir, and (Jeanne Gabrielle) Marguerite Marie, Vicomtesse Le Pelley du Manoir. George was one of eight siblings—five sisters and three brothers. His brother Yves du Manoir (1904–1928) was a famous rugby player who died tragically in an airplane accident as a young man. A French stadium and street bear his name. Another brother, Alain, became a noted writer.[2]

Count George Le Pelley du Manoir in Miami Beach, circa 1931. *George Le Pelley du Manoir (GLPDM) Papers, author's collection.*

While George du Manoir was not as wealthy as some of his relatives, he knew how to earn a living and was highly intelligent, having been educated in Switzerland, England and France and holding more than one degree from the University of Paris. Enamored with aviation, as he found it "most thrilling," for two and a half years during the First World War he flew as a machine gunner for the French government and then with the Franco-

American Aviation Corps. Later, he taught prospective pilots at the Ecole d'Aviation à Cazaux.[3]

Du Manoir made friends quickly in New York City, and on December 28, 1926, after moving to 161 Madison Avenue, he declared his intent of becoming a United States citizen. Hoping to score during the ongoing stock market boom, he worked as a securities trader, but the stock market crashed in 1929, and du Manoir had to find a job. After receiving his American pilot's license in California in 1930, he worked for the aeronautic industry and made airport inspection tours across the United States.[4]

As the weather turned colder in October, du Manoir accepted the invitation to visit his wealthy friends Robert and Evelyn Chew Gifford, who owned a large home in Miami Beach. South Florida held the promise of a warm winter vacation surrounded by affluent society, the kind of people du Manoir often encountered from years of continental travel among the bluebloods of Europe.[5]

Du Manoir decided to fly to Florida in his own airplane, a late 1920s British Whittelsey Avian with an eighty-horsepower Cirrus engine, which he kept at the Red Bank, New Jersey airport. On October 18, 1930, "wrapped in nothing more than newspapers and a delightful accent," the count headed southward in this aircraft, jokingly described as "something between a windmill and an egg crate."[6]

Flying over the Atlantic in fog as thick as vichyssoise, du Manoir heard the sputter of engine trouble, but to his relief, the skies soon cleared, and he spotted a strip of coastline in the distance. He managed to make an emergency landing at the Atlantic City airport, and when the crew rushed out to greet him, he informed them that he was Count George du Manoir from Paris. Flabbergasted, they couldn't figure out how such a rickety plane had brought the count all the way from France. Du Manoir, however, wondered how he ever managed to make it all the way from Red Bank.[7]

After mechanics fixed the engine, du Manoir continued on his journey until bad magnetos (electrical generators) forced him to land again. In fact, he made six forced landings, including one after holes in the wings caused the plane to flip over on its back in a North Carolina cotton field. He patched the damaged wings with adhesive tape, sent the bad magnetos to New York, waited for them to repair and return them and off he flew again until conditions compelled him to land on the Seminole Golf Club in Juno Beach, Florida. With a veteran flyer's luck, however, he soon took off yet again, and on January 25, 1931, he touched down at Viking Airport on the Venetian Causeway between Miami and Miami Beach.[8]

Du Manoir may have come to Miami Beach on January 25, but he did not *arrive* until two days later, when Robert Gifford introduced him to the Committee of 100 during their meeting at the home of Garfield "Gar" Wood (1880–1971). A multimillionaire motorboat builder, hydraulic lift developer, inventor and racer, Wood was a significant member of the committee and the community.[9]

Formed in Miami Beach by prominent men after the 1926 hurricane, the Committee of 100 wished not only to mingle exclusively but also to improve cultural, philanthropic, civic and economic conditions in the area and to engage the residents of Miami Beach in doing so as well. The first president was author and newspaper editor Clayton Sedgwick Cooper, and some of the earliest participants included tire magnate Harvey Samuel Firestone Sr. (1868–1938); iconic creator of Miami Beach Carl Graham Fisher (1874–1939); Miami Beach pioneer, developer and hotel builder Thomas Jessup Pancoast (1865–1941); doctor, inventor and cereal king John Harvey Kellogg; and du Manoir's host, Robert W. Gifford—a founding member.[10]

In 1930, the Committee of 100 held its first annual picnic at the Cocolobo Cay Club, built on land previously purchased by Carl Fisher and located on Adams Key, an island just off the South Florida coast (now part of Biscayne National Park). Robert Gifford brought du Manoir to the second annual picnic on the weekend of January 31, 1931, when gentlemen—dressed in jackets, ties and straw fedoras, or naval or golf caps—arrived in twenty-five signal flag–draped yachts embarking from Miami Beach's Flamingo Hotel docks. A multitude of yachts docked in Miami Beach at that time—more than in Palm Beach.[11]

During the outing, the esteemed businessmen returned to their carefree boyhood days. They ate popcorn, peanuts and hot dogs; participated in an archery tournament; and watched entertainment by African American singers, dancers, swimmers, musicians, wrestlers and boxers, described as "dusky" and "natives."[12]

Du Manoir and Gar Wood were introduced to the crowds, along with London doctor Jack Roberts. Photographers captured Roberts eating hot dogs with du Manoir, reportedly their first taste of the American delicacy.[13]

Well-known Miami Beach artist Henry Salem Hubbell brought his friend and colleague George Elmer Browne from New York City to join in the Cocolobo Cay festivities, but Hubbell did not invite his lovely wife, Rose. Indeed, according to du Manoir, these Cocolobo outings were usually "stag" affairs. In fact, some of the only times wives were permitted to events held by the Committee of 100 were balls, dinner dances and at their

Celebrities and Socialites in the Heyday of Chic

Right: Gar Wood. *Bain News Service, courtesy Library of Congress, Prints and Photographs Division.*

Below: Yachts at the Flamingo Hotel, Miami Beach, circa 1928. *State Archives of Florida.*

Vintage Miami Beach Glamour

Boxers entertain the Committee of 100 yachting picnic at the Cocolobo Cay Club, circa 1931. *Photograph by Willits, GLPDM Papers, author's collection.*

George du Manoir and British doctor Jack Roberts eating hot dogs at the Committee of 100 picnic, Cocolobo Cay Club, February 4, 1931. *Acme Newspictures, author's collection.*

"Ladies' Nights," which sometimes included talks by notables followed by a moonlit patio supper.[14]

After the 1931 picnic, du Manoir and Gifford returned to his spacious 4354 Alton Road home equipped with a staff of four catering to their every wish. Gifford, almost two decades older than the thirty-four-year-old count, and his wife, Evelyn, about forty-five, enjoyed du Manoir's engaging company and liked him even more in the following weeks. It didn't hurt that he played tennis and bridge with Robert Gifford, which improved Gifford's skills, and drove the couple to social events, as neither of them operated an automobile.[15]

In May 1931, the count returned to New York, where he boarded at a midtown hotel, but during the summer, the Giffords hosted him at their home in Spring Lake, New Jersey, where several of the Miami Beach elite socialized.[16] The following year, the Giffords toured Europe with du Manoir, and he reciprocated their hospitality by inviting them to his family home in France.[17]

Virtually adopted by the Giffords, du Manoir became the couple's protégé. He later joked that he was like the "Man Who Came to Dinner"—arriving for a brief visit and staying for around twenty-five years. While some may have called the count a titled freeloader, he earned an income through selling real estate and was so agreeable that the Giffords couldn't imagine their lives without him. In turn, du Manoir genuinely liked the Giffords and couldn't envision his life without Miami Beach.[18]

Chapter 2
THE FASHIONABLE LIFE AT PRIVATE CLUBS, HOTELS AND PARTIES

Called a bon vivant, raconteur and playboy, du Manoir may have earned a living through real estate, but high society was his life. At five-foot-six, his charm outsized his height, and his suave personality and bona fide title endeared him to Miami Beach's exclusive club coterie. In fact, during the 1930s through the 1950s, the count made so many fashionable friends in Miami Beach and Palm Beach that he wished he were twins so he could attend all the private events in both areas. Some socialites had trouble pronouncing his name—they called him "Man-oar" instead of "Man-wahhr," and one gentleman could not manage pronouncing it at all, so he simply called him "Richelieu." Nevertheless, du Manoir was "in" and stayed in.[19]

Prominent socialite Jane Fisher (1885–1968), Carl Fisher's ex-wife, instantly became a good friend of du Manoir's and remained his close ally for decades. The two had a strong rapport and enjoyed each other's sense of humor.[20]

After Carl Fisher developed Miami Beach from a jungle swamp into a fabulous resort in the 1910s and early '20s, Jane became a leader of the millionaire winter colony, charming everyone with her beautiful smile and lively personality. She inspired women to don skimpier bathing suits—cut at the knee with no long black hose—which gave them more freedom to swim but simultaneously gave Miami Beach publicists the opportunity to photograph bathing beauties showing more cheesecake.[21]

A stylish woman, Jane Fisher's stunning likeness in a Jean Patou shift was rendered in 1923 by the darling of society portraitists, Howard Chandler

Celebrities and Socialites in the Heyday of Chic

Jane Fisher, "leader of the millionaire social set," drives in Miami Beach, 1920s. *National Photo Company, author's collection.*

Christy (1872–1952). That year, Christy exhibited his work at Miami Beach's Nautilus Hotel, and on January 13, 1924, the *Miami Herald* featured her portrait by Christy on the front page of its Miami Beach section. By 1930, Christy and his wife had become members of the Bath Club.[22]

Fisher loved her likeness by Christy, posed with it in later years and bequeathed the painting to the Miami Beach Public Library and Historical Society. Although she had gone on to other marriages and divorces, she specified in her will (in which she left her son, John Warner Johnson, one dollar) that the painting be hung alongside one of "my late husband Carl Graham Fisher." Jane Fisher's portrait is presently in the collection of the fascinating HistoryMiami Museum.[23]

Aside from socializing with Fisher and other members of Miami Beach's exclusive crowd, du Manoir continued to sell real estate. He also regularly

Vintage Miami Beach Glamour

Still glamorous in a Christian Dior embroidered dress, Jane Fisher poses with her Howard Chandler Christy portrait, 1953. *Miami News Collection, HistoryMiami Museum, 1989-011-20761.*

supported the aviation industry; for instance, in the 1930s, the count served on the committee of the Aviation Ball, along with such prominent Miami Beach citizens as Robert Gifford, Clayton Sedgwick Cooper, Alfred I. Barton and Thomas J. Pancoast. The yearly event took place at the Biltmore Country Club and was held in accordance with the annual Miami All-American Air Maneuvers, sanctioned by the U.S. Army Air Corps, Navy and Marines.[24]

Despite all this activity, du Manoir, who loved everything about Miami Beach, helped promote it in articles beginning in the 1930s: "Remarkable for its pleasant climate during the winter months, unequalled for the variety of its attractions, unique for its convenient proximity of such foreign atmosphere as afforded by the Bahama Islands, Cuba, Jamaica, Venezuela, Colombia, Panama, etc., dazzling in its voluptuous tropical beauty, Miami Beach has become in recent years the winter playground of America."[25] He also found time to write other articles, some facetiously subtitled "Associated Press," and a few for a magazine called *The Gondolier*, available at hotels for Miami Beach tourists. Additionally, he wrote aviation-themed pieces for *The Sportsman Pilot*, sketches for French periodicals and commentaries simply for his own and his friends' enjoyment. The bulk of his writings from the late 1940s was likely dispersed among club members in newsletters that have been lost over the decades.[26]

Frequenting all the Miami Beach private clubs where much of the entertaining and party-giving occurred, du Manoir enjoyed the refined or raucous atmosphere and for the most part was discreet when sharing his specific observations and/or names of badly behaving members. For instance, in describing a drunken male club member who punched a guest until others pinned him down, the count wrote, "One prominent socialite, who went off the wagon...did make a short-lived display of pugilistic ardor. But he was promptly subdued and the incident passed practically unnoticed."[27]

In another essay concerning a suspected unfaithful spouse, du Manoir did not mention the name of a "flirtatious wife, whose husband had put detectives on her trail." However, this veiled reference had its consequences—no fewer than six panicked women telephoned the count thinking he was referring to them. "My! What a guilty conscience will do," he exclaimed.[28]

In yet another article, du Manoir wrote that he spotted a friend who was acting surreptitiously at a Miami Beach hotel. When the count asked him if he was in hiding from the sheriff, he responded, "Oh, George! It is much worse than that. I am in hiding from my wife!"[29]

Du Manoir also left out the names of two rambunctious houseguests of a prominent Miami Beach woman. Tired of her stinginess when it came to serving drinks, the women finished off a quart of scotch in her absence. When she returned, she overheard one of them drunkenly telling the other how she could steal the hostess's attractive husband. The next morning, the hostess asked the would-be husband-snatcher to leave, but the guest had no idea why since she had no memory of the entire episode.[30]

One of the private clubs du Manoir often visited as a guest of the Giffords was the previously cited Bath Club. The count deemed it a unique, elegant and ultraconservative organization that retained a select membership with the most impeccable manners and dress. He added that "the spectacle of this distinguished group of people…enjoying themselves with dignity made an enchanting scene too rarely held in these days of loud and gaudy merry-making."[31]

At first planned to be called the Beach Club, the Bath Club was modeled after Palm Beach's Bath and Tennis Club and opened in January 1928. Its roster comprised numerous charter members, but only a few of the stockholders actually controlled it.[32]

The Bath Club offered art classes, and one could dine and dance outside on a walled-in patio. Aside from dinner and dancing, it hosted entertainment by professional singers and dancers, such as Julie Van Zandt, whose career later included television and film. Women were eligible to join; du Manoir wrote that Emily Battelle Offutt was one of the most popular members, and founding member Lucille Mellon Hasbrouck often hosted parties that could be quite extravagant.[33]

Notwithstanding the count's respect for the Bath Club, one of du Manoir's favorites was the Surf Club. According to Alfred Ilko Barton (1892–1980), the club's secretary and vice president, the Bath Club was so packed that it could not accommodate his many friends, so he formed the Surf Club. However, Barton was not among the originators of the idea of a new and larger social gathering place. Edward Nicoll Dickerson and other notable Committee of 100 members, including Harvey S. Firestone, Carl Fisher (who built Montauk's Surf Club in 1927) and Gar Wood, first planned a more spacious nonprofit, entirely member-owned organization.[34]

The savvy Barton, however, took the dream forward and made it a reality. After the men purchased land north of the Bath Club in Surfside on the ocean, Barton promoted the idea to his large circle of socialites and bigwigs whom he knew from Philadelphia and South Florida. He assured one of his acquaintances—a baroness—that no African Americans or Jews would be allowed to join. Later, however, exceptions to that repugnant rule occurred; for instance, when a Guggenheim became a member.[35]

CELEBRITIES AND SOCIALITES IN THE HEYDAY OF CHIC

Detail, aerial view of Miami Beach showing the Bath Club, opened in January 1928. *Wendler Collection, State Archives of Florida.*

Bath and Tennis Club, Palm Beach, designed in 1926 by Joseph Urban. *Vintage postcard by Gottchalk, author's collection.*

Vintage Miami Beach Glamour

Aerial view of the Surf Club, circa 1930s. *Wendler Collection, State Archives of Florida.*

Barton, Dickerson, Biscayne Bank president James H. Gilman and other financiers, along with automobile industry magnates, formed a committee and announced that the Surf Club would be made up of one hundred founding members. They hired architect Russell Pancoast (grandson of Miami Beach's pioneer investor John Collins), who started construction in the fall of 1929 and completed the club in 1930.[36]

The Surf Club had double-decker cabanas, a saltwater pool, several tennis courts, a salon and an ample dining room and lounge connected to an enclosed loggia. The entire indoor space could accommodate well over seven hundred guests. Artist Denman Fink, who helped build Coral Gables and the University of Miami, and whose superlative work graced the walls of St. Francis Hospital and many other Miami-area public buildings and private homes, was hired to paint murals in the Surf Club's dining room.[37]

It was then up to Alfred Barton to make the club as fabulous as it looked. Born to a socialite mother in Lehigh County, Pennsylvania, and later moving to Philadelphia, Barton had spent time at private clubs and parties in Palm Beach, so he knew what pleased the very wealthy. He made the Surf Club's luxurious relaxation paramount by employing a legion of cabana boys to cater to beachgoers' whims and spared no expense on the finest food, drink and entertainment. He invented a signature cocktail, the Mangareva;

Celebrities and Socialites in the Heyday of Chic

Surf Club foyer with vaulted ceilings and cast-iron chandeliers, circa 1930. *Photograph by Claude Matlack, Photograph Album Collection, HistoryMiami Museum, X-2211-20.*

Surf Club dining room, circa 1930, showing the mural by Denman Fink. *Photograph by Claude Matlack, Photograph Album Collection, HistoryMiami Museum, X-2211-10.*

Alfred I. Barton at Hialeah Park, 1953. *Photograph by Bert Morgan, Bert Morgan Collection, HistoryMiami Museum, 2016-248-230.*

married a glamorous, socially connected wife in 1939 (Sallie Cobb "Cobbie" Johnson Jones—they divorced in 1943); and spent decades as the club's guiding force.[38]

At the start of the season, the Surf Club would hold an opening luncheon at the casual, oceanfront Mediterranean Grill, and after lunch, members would sunbathe at their cabanas.[39] Du Manoir relished sunning himself at the club and enjoyed observing others—especially females—swim. He recalled that during a particular rough, windy day, a young woman who had been bathing in the ocean stood up in the shallow waters when a "naughty big wave broke over her back and washed off the top of her suit in such fast and gentle manner that the young and beautiful lady, unaware of what had happened, remained as cool and collected as a native Balinese, until her startled husband rushed to her help."[40]

Du Manoir also enjoyed observing several other women members of the Surf Club, including a beautiful widow named Helen Anderson, who joined after her husband died. The lovely Joan Gentry, whom du Manoir described as one of the southern belles in Miami Beach, was an exceedingly popular member of the Surf Club, as well as the Indian Creek and La Gorce clubs. Often approached by "wolves," Gentry hailed from Atlanta and had been a budding singer/actress signed with Twentieth Century Fox in Hollywood. In the summer of 1946, she made an appearance at New York's Stork Club, and to honor her, in December that year candy/restaurant heir George Schrafft and his then-wife, Brownie, threw Gentry a party at the Surf Club.[41]

Another female Surf Club member in her own right, as well as a member of the Indian Creek Country Club, was "gorgeous" Phyllis Igleheart (later Lewis and then Kerdasha), whom du Manoir admired very much. Also frequently surrounded by "wolves," Phyllis contributed to the arts, designed interiors and, according to du Manoir, while in Rome appeared in the film *Quo Vadis?* Igleheart's ancestors founded Evansville, Indiana, and established Igleheart Brothers, a mill that created and sold the popular Swans Down Cake Flour. General Foods bought the company in the 1920s, and thanks to

Celebrities and Socialites in the Heyday of Chic

At the Giffords' cabana, Surf Club, December 31, 1934. *Back*: James Eben, the Giffords' New Jersey friend, and Count George du Manoir. *Front*: Robert and Evelyn Gifford. *Acme Photo, author's collection.*

Phyllis, the Igleheart family mansion and grounds would later become the Igleheart Arboretum Botanical Gardens and Bird Sanctuary.[42]

Du Manoir explained that if a woman joined the Surf Club through marriage and then divorced her husband, she would likely no longer be a member. However, there were exceptions; for example, Jane Fisher was a prominent member. Also, some three years after Alfred Barton's divorce from Sallie Cobb "Cobbie" Barton in 1943, he threw her a "welcome back to Miami Beach" party at the Surf Club, and she subsequently attended many events there.[43]

Cobbie Barton was fortunate because her ex-husband threw lavish Surf Club parties that included champagne and mounds of imported caviar, "sprinkled with egg yolk and scrapped onions… spread thick on thin, crispy melba toasts" and sumptuous suppers served to at least one hundred and sometimes as many as eight hundred guests.[44] A luncheon for the Kentucky Derby consisted of not only mint juleps but also petite marmite, pompano, strawberry soufflé and Chormel—half champagne, half Rhine wine, mixed with the liqueurs curacao and cointreau and poured into a tall glass with a peach half in it. This was followed by café au lait, crème brûlée and brandy. Guests at that gathering included art collector and philanthropist Walter P. Chrysler Jr. and wife; president of Hialeah Park John C. Clark and his spouse; and Russell and Dorothy Firestone.[45]

Joan Gentry. *Park Madison photo, from the Miami News, January 27, 1949.*

Barton's other fabulous Surf Club events could consist of trains, Ferris wheels, cowboys on rearing horses and whatever else it took to cause a sensation. Barton even replicated a stunning aurora borealis for an Alaska-themed ball. His "Big Top" party, according to du Manoir, was a highlight of the season and "the most fantastic brainchild of" Barton's, in which he turned the Surf Club into a circus. After dinner, acrobats, horses, bicyclists, female skaters, "trained dogs and love birds, clowns, side-shows" and elephants performed on the patio. Du Manoir remarked, "No wonder that particular gala attracts so many guests!"[46]

In 1949, Barton created the "Bonanza Suite" at the Surf Club, a replication in three rooms of a late nineteenth-century "Golden Nugget" saloon, complete with a "gaudy bar," authentic furniture and accessories and accompanied by old-fashioned songs, dances and costumed servers.[47] Aside from his organizational skills, design sense and event-hosting talents, Barton amassed an important collection of southwestern textiles that he later donated to the Lowe Art Museum at the University of Miami.[48]

CELEBRITIES AND SOCIALITES IN THE HEYDAY OF CHIC

In the twenty-first century the Surf Club became the stunning Four Seasons Hotel at the Surf Club, which restored the club's historic elements. Of course, all mid-twentieth-century restrictions have been banished.[49]

Reportedly, du Manoir was a member of the Indian Creek Country Club (aka Indian Creek Golf Club) for a time and golfed there with many other socialites.[50] Designed by superlative South Florida architect Maurice Fatio in 1930, the beautiful club is still situated on Indian Creek Island across a bridge from Surfside, along with several magnificent homes around the isle's perimeter. Fatio built the club with luxurious features; for instance, a men's locker room resembling a palatial hall beneath vaulted ceilings. He also designed the home of one of the club's founding members and du Manoir's friend, Harold S. Matzinger of Merrill Lynch, who had married a partner of the firm's sister and then wedded the ex-wife of a Guggenheim.[51] According to the count, the club went bankrupt in the early 1930s, but its president, David Molloy, reorganized it and remained at the helm until 1949, when he relinquished his position to William M. Orr.[52]

Champion golfers who have played the Indian Creek course include the renowned Bobby Jones, who enjoyed teeing off with Robert T. "Bob"

"View from the golf course, Indian Creek Golf Club." From *Town & Country*, February 1, 1932, 29. *Courtesy Historical Society of Palm Beach County and Hearst Publications.*

Vintage Miami Beach Glamour

"Men's Locker Room, Indian Creek Golf Club." From *Town & Country*, February 1, 1932, 28. *Courtesy Historical Society of Palm Beach County and Hearst Publications.*

Celebrities and Socialites in the Heyday of Chic

"Swimming Pool, Indian Creek Golf Club." From *Town & Country*, February 1, 1932, 30. *Courtesy Historical Society of Palm Beach County and Hearst Publications.*

Barnett, the club's popular golf pro from 1930 until his death in 1949. A vice president of the Professional Golfers' Association of America, Barnett was born in Philadelphia in 1893 and became a leading golfer in the Main Line area. He then worked at the Chevy Chase Club near Washington, D.C., and, during the summers before coming to Miami Beach, taught such notables as Presidents Warren G. Harding and William Howard Taft.[53]

On Sunday evenings at the Indian Creek Country Club, one could dine and dance on the terrace with a view of Biscayne Bay and the Miami skyline. Bachelors and debutantes mingled among some of the most prominent socialites, who would entertain the lucky young guests at their tables.[54] As for grand parties, they held a special Spinsters Ball on Christmas Eve, a Bachelors Ball on New Year's Eve and a "Hearts and Flowers" gala on Valentine's Day, complete with lavish decorations, fish and filet mignon courses, heart-shaped lobster en croute and ice cream hearts pierced with silver arrows.[55]

At some Miami Beach parties, du Manoir limited himself to one glass of Moët & Chandon, as he liked to experience the event with a clear mind. He would often scoop a wallflower standing near the band and whirl her around the dance floor. An expert at dancing, he took pleasure in it and judged competitions in waltz and rumba. The best rumba dancers were usually visitors from Cuba.[56]

Of course, the count utilized parties to network—for his real estate business and extensive social life. At a particular Miami Beach gathering, Helen Rich, one of the most elegant South Florida society columnists of her time, noticed a Palm Beach society woman bragging about her horses and polo fields to the gentleman seated next to her. As du Manoir was seated next to Rich instead of the wealthy socialite, Rich and the count decided that next time they would switch place cards so he could get better acquainted with such a valuable asset.[57]

During the season, several fancy-dress balls and costume parties took place at the clubs, private homes and hotels. The Miami Beach crowd took their costuming seriously. An invitation made it clear—either arrive in a costume or stay home—and nobody stayed home. Authenticity was so important that a woman dressed as a hula dancer refused to adorn herself with a lei made of tropical Florida blossoms and instead had flowers flown in from Hawaii. Aside from Hawaiian, Middle Eastern or Asian influences, other popular costumes of the 1930s and '40s were eighteenth-century French or Venetian, Mae West, Prince Aly Khan and screen goddess Rita Hayworth and anything inspired by the American West or Mexico.[58]

For the Committee of 100's Venetian Ball at the Nautilus Hotel in 1930, Thomas J. Pancoast manned the advisory board and dressed as a Venetian doge. A prominent developer of Miami Beach and the son-in-law of John Collins, Pancoast was secretary-treasurer and managed the Miami Beach Improvement Company, served as mayor of Miami Beach from 1918 to 1920 and was president of other Miami Beach organizations—all stressful jobs—but in costume, he could relax and enjoy himself.[59]

In 1931, du Manoir attended the third annual Oriental Ball at the Bath Club, which offered snake charmers, bronzed guards holding spears and fortunetellers. Evelyn Gifford costumed herself as a harem girl, and Robert Gifford, the club's president, dressed as a sheik, complete with a white turban.[60]

During the 1940s, the Committee of 100 continued to socialize. Du Manoir reported that longtime president Mark C. Honeywell was unable to attend the 1949 meeting, but Charles V. Beeching, club secretary, "always eager to please" one's better half (aka a club member's "little woman"), made "'ladies' night' one of the most entertaining evenings of the season." That year, John Oliver La Gorce acted with his wife as co-hosts.[61]

Celebrities and Socialites in the Heyday of Chic

Thomas J. Pancoast dressed as a Venetian doge at the annual Committee of 100 ball in Miami Beach, 1930. *Acme Newspictures, author's collection.*

La Gorce (1880–1959), a leading figure of the National Geographic Society, was such a good friend of Carl Fisher's that Fisher named a Miami Beach island after him, where several of du Manoir's friends lived, including yachtsman Cleveland Putnam and his wife, Jean. La Gorce and former Ohio governor James M. Cox established La Gorce Country Club, which opened in 1927. During the Second World War, conditions forced the city to take it over as a public golf club, but in 1945, a group of wealthy investors, including La Gorce, Cox, William "Bill" Pawley and other avid golfers and civic-minded gentlemen, spent $1 million to take it over and revert it back to a private facility. By 1948, La Gorce and Pawley were still at the helm.[62]

Such golf greats as Walter Hagen, Gene Sarazen and Jewish PGA champion Herman Barron have played at La Gorce Country Club. Nevertheless, like several other South Florida clubs formed in the early twentieth century, La Gorce restricted its membership, reflecting John La Gorce's racist and anti-Semitic temperament. Reportedly, the club had eased those antiquated limitations by the early twenty-first century.[63]

Vintage Miami Beach Glamour

Another gathering place du Manoir liked was the Quarterdeck Club, built in 1940 by Commodore Edward Turner on an enormous barge in Biscayne Bay and comprising a dining room, bar and dock slips large enough for yachts. Near Stiltsville, where homes and shacks sat atop stilts in the "flats" or shallow waters, membership was by invitation only. The count was invited for lunch there by Baron and Baroness Limnander van Nieuwenhove, who docked their yacht the *Sea King* at a Quarterdeck slip. *Life* magazine called the club "oceanic heaven" and illustrated pictures of comely bathing-suited young women fishing off the deck.[64]

In January 1949, Harold Clark Jr. took over the club and transformed it into a more exclusive "meeting place for distinguished yachtsman." The inaugural party for the revamped club was stag only and thrown by polo player Jules Romfh—the son of Miami civic leader/banker Edward Romfh—in honor of Jules's polo-playing buddy Leonard "Len" Bernard. Presumed to allow gambling, the club was raided by police in May 1949, but they could find no gaming evidence.[65]

From the 1930s through the '50s, fashion shows were often held in Miami Beach, Miami and Coral Gables. The popular store Burdine's sponsored an annual formal Sunshine Fashions show at Miami Beach's Roney Plaza, in which fifty top models dressed in the latest resort styles walked the runway, accompanied by a twelve-piece orchestra. The event originated by 1930, in concert with Burdine's shop at the hotel, and by 1933, the yearly shows had been presented with two performances—one in the afternoon and the other in the evening. Of course, with top New York fashion publications and manufacturers invited as guests, the shows promoted Burdine's line of seasonal clothing nationally. Formal fashion extravaganzas were also held at Miami Beach's Flamingo Hotel and at the Biltmore in Coral Gables.[66]

Directed by clothing and cosmetics leader Elizabeth Arden and, beginning in the late 1940s, by Doris Crane, the owner of a Miami modeling school and agency, the Surf Club weekly informal Wednesday fashion show luncheons at first were not open to men, but attracted by the glamorous models, they eventually gained access. The husbands, whom du Manoir facetiously called fashion experts, would sometimes sit apart from their wives and ask models to pause and linger by their tables. The wives didn't mind; they preferred to be separated from their spouses so they could discuss the clothes privately without criticism about prices from their husbands.[67]

Aside from fashion shows, fancy-dress balls, cocktail parties, luncheons, dinners and tennis and golf championships, Miami Beach clubs offered backgammon and bridge tournaments. They strived to attract the Palm Beach

Celebrities and Socialites in the Heyday of Chic

Burdine's Sunshine Fashions show at the Roney Plaza, Miami Beach, February 3, 1933. *Acme Newspictures, author's collection.*

Fashion show models pose on the beach at the Surf Club, circa 1945. *South Florida Photograph Collection, HistoryMiami Museum, X-1360-1.*

set, and competitions were often held between rivaling teams from Miami's Surf Club and Palm Beach's Bath and Tennis and Everglades Clubs.[68]

Du Manoir reported amusing anecdotes about some of the players' unsportsmanlike behavior during a bridge tournament at one of Miami Beach's "swankiest clubs": "Three sobbing ladies left the club…and were helped to their cars by sympathetic cabana boys; one husband threatened to kill his wife and she boldly dared him to; and a retired colonel accused a lawyer of having insulted him and demanded an apology." The count explained that although most of his readers enjoyed that column, a few, who thought "they recognized themselves among the ill-behaved characters, put up a loud 'squawk' and made a bid for my scalp." Some of the bridge players furious at him included a cattle owner who was ready to toss du Manoir into Biscayne Bay and a former attorney who "wanted to tie a heavy stone at the end of the rope to make sure I could not pull a 'Houdini' and escape from my imaginary watery grave." In the middle of this predicament, du Manoir received a witty note from his friend, the famous cartoonist Harold Tucker "Webby" Webster, who wrote that the count's problems were mild compared to a woman in St. Louis who shot her husband for criticizing her bidding at a bridge game.[69]

Other card games could also induce uncivilized behavior at social gatherings. At one, after cocktails and dinner, a few stragglers suggested a game of gin rummy. The players and kibitzers—those behind a player who give unwanted advice on how to play a hand—enjoyed themselves, and in the center of the table they put up a "kitty" in the amount of a sixty-dollar prize. The game went along smoothly until suddenly someone screamed that the money had vanished from the table. The hostess, noticing that one of the female kibitzers, a prominent socialite, was stealthily on her way out the front door, ran over to the larcenous guest and grabbed her wrist, whereupon the cash fell onto the floor.[70]

In 1948, Miami Beach clubwomen and men began to play a "new craze" called canasta or, as the count also called it, "canestra." No one quite knew how this card game was spelled or from where it derived exactly, except that it was somewhere in South America. Nevertheless, socialites in Miami Beach and in Palm Beach immediately formed committees to organize tournaments between the clubs in both centers.[71]

Miami Beach's private Gambridge Club offered additional bridge and backgammon tournaments, where members, such as du Manoir and the Giffords, often went. Established at the close of the 1938–39 winter season, it was located on Forty-First Street, and like other area clubs, membership would not be granted unless one was invited.[72]

Chapter 3

THE SPORTING LIFE IN AND AROUND MIAMI BEACH

Abutted by the Atlantic Ocean and Biscayne Bay, Miami Beach has always been a prime area for sailing, swimming, fishing, yachting and motorboat racing. Du Manoir enjoyed being on the water and referred to his boats, the SS *Silver Spray* and the *Bear Kat*, as yachts, although they ranged from only fifteen to twenty-one feet in length. He went deep-sea fishing with men and women in the Gulf Stream (as did Errol Flynn) or on Biscayne Bay off the edge of the Quarterdeck Club and sailed with women on the bay as well.[73]

In March 1933, du Manoir entered his runabout in the Race of All Nations, a featured contest in the twentieth annual Biscayne Regatta held by the Miami Beach Yacht Club. Each motorboat was "piloted by a well-known personage of a foreign country." Of course, the count flew the French flag, just before he became a United States citizen, which occurred in June that year. (While technically, a nobleman must relinquish his title to become an American, du Manoir continued to refer to himself as a count, as did his friends and the press.)[74]

All the pilots were weighed before the race, and officials added ballast to the lighter crafts so that boats would carry an equal amount. In the first race, du Manoir placed second behind a British captain of the navy, T.A. Rainey, who also commanded the gargantuan three-hundred-foot yacht *Nahlin* docked in Miami and belonging to multimillionaire Lady Yule of St. Albans, England, who was in the midst of a global tour. Du Manoir repeated his runner-up position in the second heat; however, he scored

Count George Le Pelley du Manoir in the Race of All Nations on Biscayne Bay. *International News Photos, Inc., February 27, 1933, author's collection.*

third in total points for the races, and as only three boats competed, he officially finished last.[75]

Du Manoir fared much better with a tennis racket. In fact, he was a well-known, successful and popular tournament player, the press deeming him as an "outstanding tennis figure" and "noted amateur tennis star."[76]

Along with his good friend, Surf Club singles champion William J. "Bill" Tully (1925–2016), du Manoir often competed at the Surf Club and Miami Beach's Nautilus Hotel, as well as Palm Beach's Bath and Tennis and Everglades Clubs. In fact, the count appeared in so many Miami Beach and Palm Beach tournaments that in the early 1930s, he flew his own plane between matches.[77]

Other Miami Beach players battled the Palm Beach club crowd on the courts. At an Everglades Club competition, du Manoir and Tully were joined by Surf Club members Don Graves and Miami Beach scientist Philip B. Hawk, who volleyed with Palm Beach real estate developer A. Parker Bryant; Palm Beach/Cincinnati attorney and civic leader Ray Kunkel; Palm Beach community and church leader William G. Cluett; Palm Beach financier and philanthropist Page Hufty; and Palm Beacher J. Spencer Love, founder of Burlington Mills.[78]

Celebrities and Socialites in the Heyday of Chic

Left: Du Manoir at the Nautilus Hotel tennis courts. *GLPDM Papers, author's collection*.

Below: Trophy presentation, Everglades Club, Palm Beach. *From left to right*: Don Graves, Bill Tully, Dr. Francis Farber, George du Manoir, Philip B. Hawk, A. Parker Bryant, Raymond Kunkel, Hunt T. Dickinson, William G. Cluett, Richard Williams, Page Hufty, David Gerli and J. Spencer Love. *Photograph by Bert Morgan, circa 1949; State Archives of Florida*.

Du Manoir also participated in tourneys throughout the nation and competed against champion amateurs, including the top-ranked Bobby Riggs (1918–1995), who later turned pro. In 1938, Wayne Sabin and Riggs, who also played at the Surf Club and Biltmore, defeated du Manoir and Prince Georges Alexandrovich Stroganoff Scherbatoff in a doubles match at the Nautilus Hotel.[79] As illustrated, Riggs already knew at the age of almost twenty how to utilize the opposite sex for self-promotion—decades before he arranged the 1973 "Battle of the Sexes" tennis match in which Billie Jean King demolished him on the court.

One of the count's successful doubles partners at the Roney Plaza courts was Bernard Baruch Jr., son of the famous statesman. Du Manoir stayed in touch with Baruch Jr., his father and his uncle, Sailing Baruch, who lived on Miami Beach's beautiful Di Lido Island. The count called Bernard Baruch Sr. and Jr. "Barney."[80]

In singles matches at Palm Beach's Bath and Tennis Club, du Manoir played against his buddy Igor Cassini, one of the popular national columnists known as Cholly Knickerbocker.[81] The count also endeared himself to such top tennis players as British physician and pacifist Archibald Adam Warden (1869–1943), who won a bronze medal at the 1900 Olympics. On December 30, 1934, Warden wrote to du Manoir at the Giffords' Alton Road address, expressing that even at sixty-six, he was playing tennis as well as he ever did before. "A five set single match is still my delight and I wish I could meet you again! My only grievance—and a real one—is the New York Stock Exchange who ran away with all my hard-earned savings. Couldn't you find a job for a young chap like me?"[82]

In 1935, du Manoir and Miami resident Searle Barnett played in a mixed doubles tournament in which Barnett, with his glamorous daughter Marta Barnett (1918–2005), placed second. Four years later, Marta married tennis player George Andrade—and divorced him in 1946.[83] She competed at Wimbledon and Forest Hills and during the 1930s was a recurring Florida State Women's Tennis champion. In 1938, she made Miami even prouder by winning the prestigious Southern Championship, and she repeated her victory in 1939. That year, she also captured the women's singles championship at the National Public Parks Tennis Tournament in New York and then posed triumphantly in Miami Beach wearing a chic leopard print ensemble.[84]

Bill Tully and du Manoir participated in the Spring Lake, New Jersey Invitational Tennis Tournament in July 1949. While Tully was playing brilliantly, a female burglar robbed his family's home in Bronxville, New York, but her misuse of his father's checkbook led to her arrest.[85] In the

Tennis champion Bobby Riggs posing with beautiful women during a break at the Biltmore courts, Coral Gables, January 1938. *Miami News Service, author's collection.*

same tournament, officials robbed du Manoir's chances at a championship when they pitted him against six-foot-three, top-seeded amateur Ricardo Alonso (Richard) "Pancho" Gonzales (1928–1995), who trounced the count 6–1, 6–2. Du Manoir wrote that he "felt very lucky to chalk 3 games to my credit against the US National Champion." Gonzales soon turned pro and became one of the greatest tennis stars in history, whose matches, aside from internationally known venues, took place in Miami Beach and Palm Beach.

Vintage Miami Beach Glamour

Tennis champion Marta Barnett posing in Miami Beach, 1939. *State Archives of Florida.*

Bill Tully went on to represent the United States in the 1968 Olympics, win twenty-two U.S. Tennis Association National Titles and become a champion senior player on the circuit as well.[86]

Sometimes tennis tournaments interfered with du Manoir's socializing. He recalled that after enjoying appetizers and cocktails at a Miami Beach gin and tonic party, where so many drinks were consumed by guests that they all would be "immune from malaria for years to come," he suddenly remembered that he was scheduled to play in a semifinal Surf Club tennis match. Fortunately, he arrived on time, played well and later exclaimed, "To my great surprise, my diet of Gin Tonics carried me through to the finals with the loss of only one game. That quinine seems to be just the thing for me!"[87]

Du Manoir playing tennis in Miami Beach. *Photograph by Verne O. Williams, George du Manoir Collection, HistoryMiami Museum.*

In 1941, du Manoir went hunting for the first time. Fortunately, two experienced sportsmen, Lawrence Romfh (Jules Romfh's brother) and Dr. B.L. Whitten, a board member of Hialeah Park, accompanied him. Du Manoir appreciated such agreeable hunters who could teach him exactly how to shoot a gun, preferably not at himself or someone else.[88]

In a typewritten article, possibly for *The Gondolier*, Du Manoir explained that he first went to the "hunting and marriage licenses" department of the courthouse and obtained a hunting license for $5.50, "very reasonable," he thought. Next, he bought equipment at a hardware store. "They even sell a double kapok mattress for two. Personally, when hunting, we like a single one, definitely."[89]

Du Manoir also advised to be careful of the hunting companions you choose, because inflammatory political conversation—especially during the volatile period just before America entered World War II—did not mix well with guns and ammunition. He warned that if you hunted with someone with an opposing opinion, there could well be an "accident" in the "wild solitude of the jungle."[90]

The men started their adventure by traveling to the small village of Immokalee, "easy to reach from Miami Beach"; simply take "Tamiami Trail to [the] Everglades: then thirty two miles north on a picturesque dirt road through the swamps and cypress forests." Du Manoir advised to find a Seminole guide, and when he leads you into the Everglades, you should "be quick on the trigger, and you will have the fun of your life."[91]

While some other hunting parties stalked deer, panthers and alligators, du Manoir and his friends hunted for quail, snipe and wild geese. Their truck was equipped with a large refrigerator, and for assistance, they brought five pointers and one retriever. They forged through swamps, ran across fields and over fences and fought their way through dense palmettos until the dogs were exhausted and the men were satisfied with their ample quarry. Dinner around the campfire consisted of "a good hot soup, a few juicy broiled quails, a baked Idaho potato and a salad of hearts of palmetto. What a meal!!!!"[92]

The count relished the Everglades and returned often to hunt, fish and enjoy nature. However, it always felt good to return to the pleasures and luxury of Miami Beach.

Chapter 4

MIAMI BEACH PERSONALITIES

THE HIGH-FLYING DU PONTS, TALENTED FIRESTONES AND THE REMARKABLE SHIRLEY COWELL

In January 1934, du Manoir put his airplane on the market, listing it at $800 with an overhauled motor, but he lowered the price to $600 in July. Fortunately, the plane came equipped with a parachute at no extra charge.[93]

The following year, the count wrote an essay about two aviators he admired, Richard Chichester du Pont (1911–1943) and his cousin Éleuthère Paul du Pont Jr. (1911–1963). They both wintered frequently in Miami Beach, "away from their snow covered home state of Delaware."[94]

Richard and Paul du Pont were members of one of the wealthiest and most philanthropic families in the United States, who originally made their fortune in gunpowder. Of course, the DuPont company later became renowned for manufacturing iconic synthetic materials.

According to du Manoir, the du Pont seniors were hardworking and the well-known juniors were high flying: "Both are famous for their activities in the field of aviation, and after the fashion of the Man on the Flying trapeze, only more so, 'they fly and glide through the air with the greatest of ease.'"[95]

But the younger du Ponts worked hard as well. Gliding pioneer racer and world record holder Richard du Pont founded All American Aviation, which became USAir. The dashing E. Paul du Pont Jr. was also an avid glider and record-holder in the sport. He invented a glider and worked at the DuPont company but later established his own businesses.[96]

On March 19, 1934, Richard du Pont, who often stayed at the Nautilus Hotel while in town, married Helena Allaire Crozer. A champion pilot in

Engaged couple Richard du Pont and Helena Allaire Crozer at the Miami Municipal Airport, sixth annual Air Meet, January 1934. *Associated Press photograph, author's collection.*

Jack O'Meara, E. Paul du Pont Jr. (*center*) and Elwood Klein, just before taking off on the "sky train" flight. *From the* Miami News, *May 14, 1935.*

women's races, Allaire's socially prominent parents from Philadelphia owned a house in Miami.[97]

The following year, Paul du Pont, at only around twenty-four years of age, along with Jack O'Meara and Elwood Klein, made the first international "sky train" flight. The "train" consisted of an airplane towing two gliders from Miami to Key West and Havana, Cuba. O'Meara manned the first glider; du Pont piloted the second one; and Klein was the pilot of the tow plane.[98]

Thousands of people in Havana turned out to see the sky train emerge from above on May 14, 1935. Quivering with excitement and applauding thunderously, they watched intently as the three aircraft came into view and landed in perfect order before the Cuban capitol. Planned to be a round-trip affair, the sky train returned triumphantly to Miami after a few days in Havana. The entire event commemorated the May 17, 1913 first trip by air from Key West to Havana, and the Cuban government issued a special airmail stamp sent to the United States to honor the 1935 historic flight.[99]

During the 1930s, Richard or Paul du Pont flew Allaire du Pont's sister, Marion Crozer, from Viking Airport on the Venetian Causeway to New York and vice versa. Du Manoir was especially fond of Crozer, who often accompanied him to various Miami Beach clubs and events. Sometimes they socialized along with Richard du Pont's sister Alice, such as at a St. Patrick's Day luncheon at Roney Plaza's Café de la Paix, and they also won mixed doubles tennis tournaments together.[100] Du Manoir described Crozer glowingly in his du Pont essay, referring to himself in the third person:

> *Miss Marion Crozer…has been a visitor in Miami Beach for the second consecutive year. Not a Tycoon, nor a Farmer; yet sensitive to the fascination of the Tropics and the consequences of the Depression, Miss Marion Crozer finds on these hospitable shores the ideal field for her social and sportive activities. Lavishly gifted with that certain charm that keeps the boys away from the farm, and that certain thing that makes the birds forget to sing, she has also received from Mother Nature a good health, a strong frame, and powerful muscles.*
>
> *Very democratic in her selection of tennis and swimming partners, she is most particular in her choice of sailing and flying companions. All her sailing is done in the company of Vicomte Georges Henri Marie Le Pelley du Manoir…proud owner and captain of the Yacht S.S. "Silver Spray" of the port of Miami Beach, Florida, 15 feet in length. All her flying is done exclusively in the select company of two members of the du Pont family.*[101]

Du Manoir then related one of Crozer's departures in Paul du Pont's plane, accompanied by her maid and pet Boston terrier, Mazurka:

> *Late last night, Miss Crozer, Paul du Pont, maid, valises, and dog drove their car to the Viking Airport and walked up to the young man's 210 H. P. Stinson, made ready for their return journey home. Stuffing the luggage in every available corner of the plane, getting everything in order for a comfortable night flight, they were delayed for several hours when the…belly of the plumpy maid…refused to be squeezed into the safety belt. With the help of six mechanics, an ice man, and two truck drivers, they were able to compress the reluctant stomach [and] stretch the belt. Not air-minded, Miss Boston Terrier Mazurka sat trembling on the red leather upholstered*

Celebrities and Socialites in the Heyday of Chic

Marion Crozer volunteering at a hospital charity event, 1933. *Acme Photo, author's collection.*

seat, [but] *saved herself from disgrace the next morning thanks to fast-thinking Miss Crozer's swift gesture. Reaching their destination at 12 noon the next day, the flyers found nasty weather at home* [and] *wished they had never left Sunshining Miami Beach.*[102]

Marion Crozer returned to Miami Beach frequently and, in 1941, dined with the count and others at an elegant beachfront hotel. The dinner was hosted by du Manoir's good friend, the renowned art collector, National Gallery philanthropist and owner of Hialeah Park Race Track Joseph E. Widener. That year, Marion married John Sailer, and du Manoir penciled the couple's new contact information in his address book.[103]

Tragically, Richard du Pont died as a passenger in an experimental glider's crash in 1943. A heartbroken Allaire joined the board of All American Aviation but never remarried because Richard was "the love of her life." A major horse breeder, she owned one of the world's greatest thoroughbreds, Kelso, and became the first woman admitted into the Jockey Club, the prestigious breed registry. A stakes race has been named after her.[104]

Du Manoir was also a good friend of Roger Stanley Firestone's; he was the youngest son of Miami Beach's prominent citizen Harvey S. Firestone Sr. (1868–1938), who owned one of the grandest mansions in the city—later the site of the Fontainebleau hotel.[105] The count noted more than once the accomplishments of Roger's brother Harvey S. Firestone Jr. (1898–1973), Firestone Tire and Rubber Company's chairman of the board. His fashion-loving wife, Elizabeth "Betty" Parke Firestone, collected extraordinary haute couture as well as *objets de vertu*.

In November 1948, du Manoir reported that Harvey Firestone Jr. won the highest medal of France, the Legion of Honor, for outstanding service to international agriculture:

> *I was particularly happy to learn that Harvey Firestone has just been decorated by the French Government. Here is a member of the smart set who works hard and carries on his shoulders heavy responsibilities. Yet, when it comes to enjoying himself, he knows how to have and give his friends a good time. It is always a pleasure to find one's self in his witty company. Well! It's good to know that the French are grateful for whatever he did for them and since the decoration was granted by mail, Harvey will not have to stand and be kissed on both cheeks by a French General. This must please him too.*[106]

Du Manoir also admired Harvey Firestone Jr.'s daughter Elizabeth Firestone (Willis) (1922–1989) when he heard her sing and play piano on the radio. A talented musician and composer, Elizabeth made her Miami Beach debut in 1943 on WKAT, and was so popular that the station invited her back many times. After plenty of practice, she performed at Carnegie Hall in 1946. Not only would Elizabeth write songs for the legendary star Lena Horne, but she would also create film scores and provide campaign music for Dwight D. Eisenhower, Richard Nixon and George H.W. Bush. In later years, jazz caught her fancy, and she appeared with such stars as B.B. King, Mel Tormé, Gene Krupa and Lionel Hampton. Her sister Martha married a descendant of Henry Ford and became the owner of the Detroit Lions.[107]

Elizabeth Firestone performs on WKAT, Miami Beach, 1943. *International News Photos, author's collection.*

Another Miami Beach woman who became a songwriter for Lena Horne—as well as Johnny Mathis and other artists—was socialite Shirley Cowell (1923–1997). The daughter of Ione Staley Cowell and granddaughter of food magnate Augustus E. Staley, who had owned a luxurious Miami house on Point View, Cowell spent winters in Miami Beach because of a chronic asthma condition. She lived in a lavish Sunset Island home formerly belonging to Howard Hughes and, when not hosting elegant parties, wrote music and lyrics while lounging beside her pool.[108]

Du Manoir admired Cowell's "effective and appealing" voice and thought she showed great promise when she made her radio debut on WGBS on February 5, 1949. He hoped that, along with her social circle, a Miami publicist or agent was listening. Singing passionately, Cowell was a hit and eventually hosted her own Miami radio show.[109] A lesbian, she later adopted her lover, model/actress Gigi Carrier Cowell, in order to endow her with a rightful inheritance.[110]

Du Manoir encountered Shirley Cowell at many social events other than her own soirees. One night, he noticed her at a hotel bar as she sipped cocktails with aspiring singer/actress Martha Elizabeth Schenck, who, the count disclosed, would soon work at a nightclub "under an assumed name."[111]

Schenck's stage name was Marti Stevens. In February 1950, Stevens sang at Club Boheme on Ocean Drive in Hallandale and subsequently became nationally successful, appearing in many prestigious clubs, on television, in movies and in theatrical productions. In 1954, she married polo player and Butler Aviation heir Michael Butler, a bisexual who, during their honeymoon, had an affair with Hollywood heartthrob Rock Hudson. Stevens's marriage lasted less than a year.[112]

In the meantime, Stevens had become an intimate friend of Marlene Dietrich's. Rampant rumors spread around Hollywood that they were lovers, but apparently, Stevens's mother, Pansy, the wife of leading Metro-Goldwyn-Mayer executive Nicholas Schenck, had no knowledge of a sexual relationship between her daughter and the movie star.[113]

One night, Pansy, Shirley Cowell and their good friend, singer Eileen Farrell, met Dietrich backstage at Miami Beach's Fontainebleau hotel. After introductions, Pansy innocently said to Dietrich, "I think you know my daughter Marti."[114]

Dietrich paused, smiled knowingly and answered, "Oh yes, I *do*."[115]

Chapter 5
A NEW VERSAILLES AND A SECOND WORLD WAR

The count dined and socialized at several Miami Beach hotels, most already mentioned: the Pancoast, Nautilus, Flamingo, Roney Plaza and King Cole. All these structures were subsequently destroyed.[116]

Du Manoir also considered a more modern hotel one of his favorites—the Versailles. At the end of December 1940, he attended the Versailles opening with five hundred other Miamians. Shortly thereafter, the count wrote about the glamorous Art Deco building on Collins Avenue at Thirty-Fourth and Thirty-Fifth Streets, designed by architect Roy F. France:[117]

> *Built at the very tip of that point of the Beach farthest east and closest to the Gulf Stream, it commands in every direction a superb view of the ocean from all its rooms. The building is of modern architecture, and modern at the best, with taste and elegance. It stands up, the highest edifice on the beach, as a monument to the skill and ingenuity of a great architect. As you look up to its original cupola, you are thrilled with a sensation of lightness and gracefulness, difficult indeed, almost impossible to achieve in a work of this importance. The lofty entrance, the vast lobby add dignity to an atmosphere of luxurious comfort.*[118]

Du Manoir called the Versailles' dining room "splendid" and noted its excellent cuisine. He also visited the wine cellar, with "so many bottles and such great names."[119] One night, after actress Mary Brian, who was starring in an area theatrical production, enjoyed lunching in the dining room, du

Vintage Miami Beach Glamour

The Versailles, Miami Beach, 1946. *Department of Commerce Collection, State Archives of Florida.*

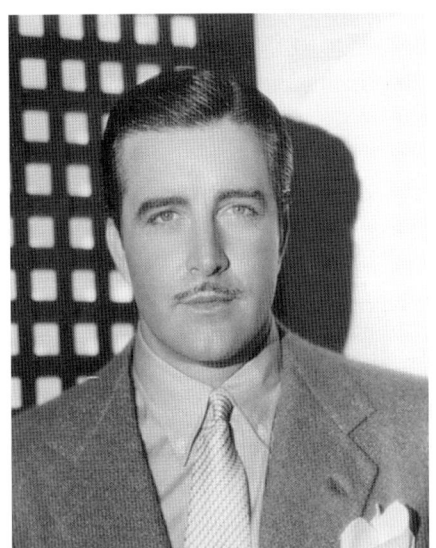

Celebrities and Socialites in the Heyday of Chic

Left: Actor and singer John Boles; *Right*: actress Mary Brian. *Glossy reprints, photographers unknown, author's collection.*

Manoir hosted friends there. Handsome actor John Boles, who starred in the iconic *Frankenstein*, *Back Street* and *Stella Dallas*, as well as a few classic films with Shirley Temple, was having his dinner at an adjacent table. Also a gifted singer, Boles was in town primarily to perform at the Olympia Theater on Flagler Street in Miami.[120]

Du Manoir and his guests experienced the finest of French food, delighted in the hotel's entertainment and appreciated the star power and finery around them. He then concluded his article: "And now that we have told you where it is and what it is, what else could we do for you but lift our glass to your good health and wish you a juicy filet mignon to the accompaniment of a perfect orchestra in full view of a wonderful floor show, and a very long and pleasant stay at the Versailles."[121]

Beginning in 2015, developers led by Alan Faena extensively renovated the Versailles. Fortunately, the façade and many of the beautiful lobby's Art Deco designs have been preserved.[122]

Meanwhile, in January 1942, du Manoir flew from New York to Miami and registered for the draft in February, listing Robert Gifford as his next of kin and Miami Beach realtor Allen M. Martin as his employer. Du Manoir was absent from the Miami papers that season and the following one as well. He spent time in Europe and, while there, obtained photographs of a

57

French nightclub where patrons, including civilians and Nazi officers, mingled closely together—uncomfortably close.[123]

During World War II, several Miami Beach hotels became hospitals. The U.S. Army Air Corps Officers Candidate School took over many other hotels and organizations, including the Surf Club, and taught such celebrity officers-in-training as Sergeant Clark Gable. The military also took control of restaurants and nightclubs, such as the Palm Island Latin Quarter, and turned them into commissaries.[124]

While golf courses became training grounds, subdued gatherings took place at private homes. The Giffords participated in a modicum of social events—some charitable. For instance, Evelyn Gifford devoted herself to the Humane Society of Greater Miami. Before the war, du Manoir had helped her in her efforts by writing at least one article praising the fine organization and asking for donations.[125]

Du Manoir returned to Florida by December 1943 and, with the Giffords and other friends, celebrated New Year's Eve at Palm Beach's Everglades Club. He looked forward to the 1944 Miami Beach season and the eventual end of the war.[126]

Sergeant Clark Gable, U.S. Army Air Corps Officers' Candidate School, Miami Beach, Squadron 13. *From Army Air Forces Yearbook 1942, Group C, Squadrons 13–18.*

Chapter 6
THE COUNT'S FRIEND HOSTS THE WINSTON CHURCHILLS

Du Manoir frequently socialized with Miami Beach winter colonist Colonel Frank Clarke, who, along with his brother Desmond, was a steamship and wood pulp magnate from Montreal, Canada. Frank Clarke's son Jim and his nephew Sanford "Sandy" Clarke were closer to du Manoir's age and also his friends. In the late 1940s, du Manoir and the Clarke family celebrated Sandy's marriage, "one of the most sensational events in the social world," to a "beautiful, irresistible" Cuban woman named Josefina Delgado.[127]

For several weeks during the 1946 winter season, Frank Clarke hosted Winston Churchill (1874–1965) and his wife, Clementine, in Clarke's Miami Beach house at 5905 North Bay Road. A good friend of Clarke's, Churchill had previously vacationed at the colonel's Canadian campgrounds following a World War II Quebec Conference.[128]

Prior to Churchill's arrival in Miami Beach, Clarke excitedly made preparations for the great leader's visit. The colonel's home, with its expansive living room, garden and glamorous Art Deco–style dining room, exuded more than enough elegance to suit Churchill, who had rather unfussy taste in accommodations. Nevertheless, Clarke gave up his master bedroom for the dignitary, and gardeners made sure no ants in the bougainvillea would bother him on the patio. The chauffer spruced up the Cadillac, flowers filled the house and scattered papers were cleared in the study in case "Winnie" might want to write a letter or work on his memoirs. Clarke's Irish cook was confident she could take good care of the Churchills and promised she

Dining room, Colonel Frank Clarke house, 5905 North Bay Road, Miami Beach, January 1946. *Acme Newspictures, author's collection.*

would "find a way to the former British prime minister's heart with plain but tasty dishes."[129]

On January 16, 1946, Churchill arrived in Miami aboard a train from New York for his long-needed vacation. The media, waiting for him at the station and the Clarke house, clamored for an interview. Swarmed by photographers, journalists and filmmakers, Clarke and the Churchills sat in the colonel's garden, and after a bit of conviviality with the press, Churchill said, "I've been asked to say just ten words, but I haven't been told which ten words they should be. But there are ten words—or thereabouts ten—which come very readily to my mind, and that is the great pleasure I have in feeling the genial sunshine of Miami Beach." He then muttered the same words while adding them up on his fingers and concluded jokingly, "One too many, one too many!"[130]

The following day, after standing on the sidewalk and waving and talking to motorists passing Clarke's home, Churchill visited Miami's Parrot Jungle, where the affectionate tropical birds perched on his shoulder and nuzzled him.[131] Subsequently, at the end of January, the Churchills attended Hialeah Park, where track president John C. Clark and his wife hosted them. Then, in the beginning of February, Frank Clarke and the couple took a side trip to Havana, Cuba, but Clarke returned to Miami Beach to meet with the Churchills' daughter Sarah, whose delayed flight had touched down just after her parents had left. Clarke drove her to the airport and accompanied her to Cuba, where she reunited with Winston and Clementine. They all returned to Miami Beach on February 10, and a few days later, Churchill received an honorary degree from the University of Miami, followed by a reception at the Surf Club.[132]

The relaxation offered at the Surf Club appealed to Churchill, who painted scenes of the coastline from Frank Clarke's cabana. So intent on rendering the club's deck, beach and the Atlantic Ocean, Churchill did not attend a tour of the clubhouse Clarke gave, but Clementine accompanied the colonel and later joined her husband in the cabana.[133] Churchill also

Winston Churchill jokingly counts on his fingers with his wife, Clementine, at Colonel Frank Clarke's house, Miami Beach, January 16, 1946. *Photographer unknown, author's collection.*

Vintage Miami Beach Glamour

Frank Clarke and Sarah Churchill in a car on North Bay Road, Miami Beach, about to drive to the airport to fly to Havana, Cuba. *Acme Newspictures, February 5, 1946, author's collection.*

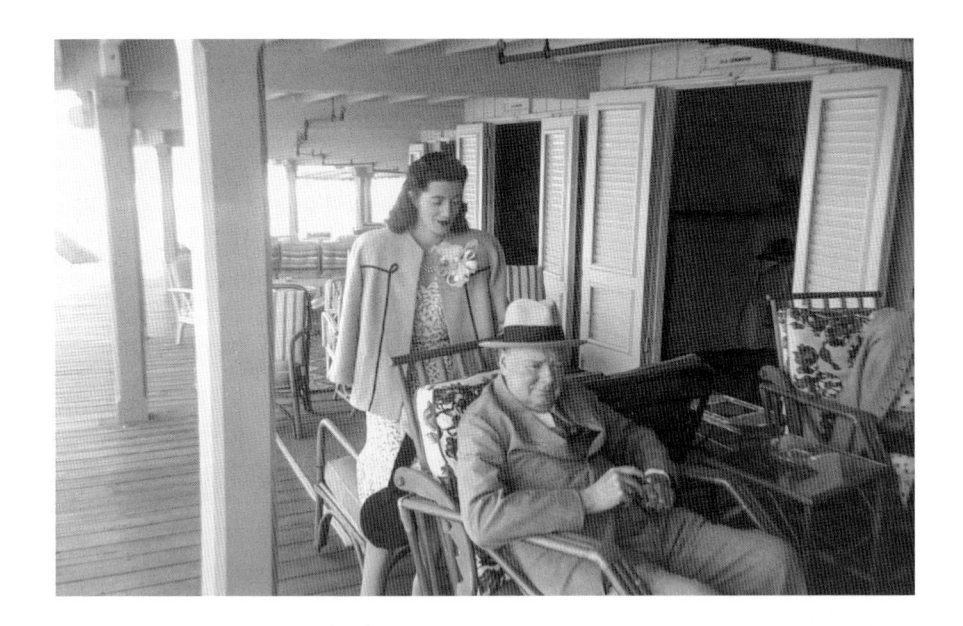

CELEBRITIES AND SOCIALITES IN THE HEYDAY OF CHIC

Above: Winston Churchill and Sarah Churchill (at the Surf Club, Surfside, just north of) Miami Beach, Florida, February 27, 1946. *KFC12N, Kennedy Family Collection. Copyright © John F. Kennedy Library Foundation.*

Right: Winston Churchill painting in Frank Clarke's cabana at the Surf Club, 1946. *State Archives of Florida.*

swam in the ocean, which he enjoyed very much. In fact, in a 1948 letter to Clarke, Churchill expressed his long-lasting, fond memories of his time swimming off the Surf Club's shore.[134]

Clementine enjoyed her stay as well; she attended a fashion show at the Surf Club and shopped for dresses on Miami Beach's posh Lincoln Road. Always gracious, she sent a thank-you note to at least one of the dress shop's owners.[135]

Writing to her youngest daughter, Mary, Clementine described South Florida's "tropical heat, rather much but delicious"; the nighttime coolness; "lovely flowering hedges of hibiscus pink lemon & apricot"; and the "heavenly" sea. She was especially interested in native foliage that made up the flower pieces decorating the Clarke home with changing themes, from formal when the couple first arrived to romantic during Valentine's Day and then soothing and casual during the rest of their stay. However, she worried when her husband caught a chill but was relieved when he recovered from the brief illness.[136]

On March 1, the last day of their visit, Churchill had a group of parrots, macaws and cockatoos brought from Parrot Jungle to Clarke's house so that Clementine and Sarah could enjoy them.[137] That evening, as a grand finale of their pleasurable time, the future Sir Winston Churchill was fêted at a farewell party at his favorite place—the Surf Club—before they left for Washington, D.C..[138]

In 1949, du Manoir reported that Churchill's second cousin and godson, John George Vanderbilt Henry Spencer-Churchill (1926–2014), the Marquess of Blandford and future eleventh Duke of Marlborough, would be making a trip to Florida. The count hoped that, like his esteemed cousin, Lord Blandford would also visit Hialeah Park before he saw his grandmother Madame Jacques Balsan, the former Consuelo Vanderbilt, Duchess of Marlborough, at her home, Casa Alva, just south of Palm Beach.[139]

Du Manoir, obtaining some of his information from the September 1949 issue of *Life* magazine, hinted that the tall, dashing Spencer-Churchill "has been reported to be one of the most intimate friends of a gay princess of royal blood." He meant Princess Margaret, whom the nobleman had escorted to Ascot; entertained at his family's castle, Blenheim; and spent time with at Balmoral castle. The two, however, did not marry.[140]

Du Manoir concluded by expressing that if Spencer-Churchill did visit Hialeah, not only would track attendees get to see a British lord in top hat and cutaway, but the marquess would have the opportunity to see the "most colorful track in the world," with its fabulous pink flamingos.[141]

Chapter 7
HIALEAH MEMORIES

During the 1930s and '40s, upper-class spectators attending Hialeah Park Race Track dressed to match its elegance. Men wore custom-made suits accompanied by pocket squares, ties and straw or felt fedoras, and women showed off chic outfits accented by stylish hats and gloves.

Du Manoir enjoyed the track and got along well with the Hialeah Park set. As mentioned, he was a friend of owner Joseph E. Widener, who, after purchasing the park, beautified it with tropical palm trees and bougainvillea. Other horse-loving friends included John C. Clark, track president from 1940 until 1955, and Charles and Dorothy Bromley. The Bromleys, from Chestnut Hill in Philadelphia, Pennsylvania, owned the prominent Cedar Farm that produced several horses stabled at Hialeah.[142]

Joseph Widener's son Peter Arrell Browne Widener II (1895–1948) was an avid horse breeder as well. During a Hialeah luncheon of lobster Newburg and chocolate éclairs, du Manoir was glad to see Peter and called him "one of the most colorful figures we have ever met," whose "wit and humour are a constant source of pleasure for his many friends."[143]

Widener's elegant wife, Gertrude, also successfully bred champion racehorses. Familiarly called "Gertie," in the 1930s she epitomized the duchess of Windsor's quip that a woman could "never be too rich or too thin." Gertrude often played hostess to the crème de la crème of Miami Beach and Palm Beach, as well as to titled European horse breeders, including Sir Humphrey de Trafford, Fourth Baronet, who was also a well-known amateur rider.[144]

Vintage Miami Beach Glamour

Closing day at Hialeah, March 2, 1941, with a total of twenty-one thousand fans attending. *Acme Newspictures, author's collection.*

CELEBRITIES AND SOCIALITES IN THE HEYDAY OF CHIC

Above: Charlotte Bromley and George du Manoir in the Bromley box at Hialeah Park, January 23, 1938. *Acme Newspictures, author's collection.*

Right: Gertrude (Mrs. Peter A.B.) Widener walks with Sir Humphrey de Trafford at Hialeah Park, January 16, 1937. *Acme Newspictures, author's collection.*

At the same Hialeah luncheon, du Manoir noticed publicist Joe Copps, "one of the most active guests present. You bet he was. He gave a masterful kiss to the most beautiful lady at the party, and received a magnificent one in exchange. Lucky Joe!!"[145]

As a fellow South Florida booster, du Manoir admired Copps, "whose brilliant publicity brings Miami Beach to the front pages of every newspaper in the forty-eight states of the union." Along with Larry Smits, Copps had joined the staff led by the legendary Steve Hannagan, foremost in promoting Miami Beach, who had worked for Carl Fisher, the City of Miami Beach, and led the Miami Beach News Bureau. Hannagan, Copps and Smits, called the "Three Musketeers," created real but inconsequential news accompanied by flashy "resort art" photographs, such as Santa Claus pulling a net from the ocean filled with bathing beauties or St. Nick standing on the beach with swim-suited women holding presents advertising Miami Beach attractions. Indeed, this kind of sunshine-soaked cheesecake was a press agent's dream to lure tourists.[146]

Du Manoir also mingled with Damon Runyon (1880–1946) and his beautiful wife, Patrice, at Hialeah Park, as well as at parties on yachts and at the Surf Club. The Runyons lived on Miami Beach's Hibiscus Island, one of several man-made islands in Biscayne Bay, and in 1935 were photographed at their house just before they left for Hialeah. A renowned New York columnist and short story writer, Runyon frequently attended the track, and his amusing tales of colorful Manhattan gamblers, show girls and bootleggers became the basis of the musical *Guys and Dolls*.[147]

Prominent leader of Palm Beach society Charles Alexander Munn (1885–1981) flew his own plane to Miami, lunched at the Surf Club and stopped by other watering holes while not viewing races from his box at Hialeah. His daughters, Frances Drexel Munn (later Mrs. George F. Baker) and Mary Munn (later the Countess of Bessborough), made good use of the prime seats, as did substantial friends, including New York philanthropist/financier William Rhinelander Stewart and his glamorous wife, Janet, who both socialized in Miami and Miami Beach.[148]

Frances "Fannie" Kesner Hertz and her husband, rental car king John D. Hertz, had a box at Hialeah as well. Friends of du Manoir's, the Hertz family lived for a time at 4901 Collins Avenue, and their daughter played tennis with the count. Mrs. Hertz owned Count Fleet, the 1943 Triple Crown winner.[149]

Additional Hialeah spectators whom du Manoir knew included "Count José Dorelis, ex-husband of the often-married Dolly Heminway

Celebrities and Socialites in the Heyday of Chic

Damon Runyon and his wife, Patrice, with their pet dog on the patio of their Miami Beach home, before heading to Hialeah Park, November 18, 1935. *International News Photos, author's collection.*

Detail, Charles A. Munn Box at Hialeah Park, 1937. *Front row*: Mary Munn, Frances Munn. *Back row*: William Rhinelander Stewart and his wife, Janet. *Miami News Service, author's collection.*

Fleischmann (as in the yeast company) O'Brien Dorelis." Dolly, who had been romantically involved with Clark Gable just after World War II, lived in Palm Beach and was a noted hostess who socialized with the Munns and Wrightsmans. The Dorelis marriage only lasted from 1946 to 1947, but life went on for both of them; José married a model, and Dolly went back to hosting parties in Palm Beach.[150]

Yet another Hialeah fan and friend of du Manoir's was Margaret "Peggy" Thayer Talbott, whose mother had survived the *Titanic* disaster. Peggy and her husband were prominent members of the horsey set from New York to

Miami and wintered at the King Cole Hotel in Miami Beach. The wife of Harold Elstner Talbott, third secretary of the air force who in 1955 would win the Medal of Freedom, Peggy made headlines of her own in 1940 when designers voted her onto the international best dressed list.[151]

On "Flamingo Day" at Hialeah, the famous Flamingo Stakes race occurred with extra entertainment; for instance, in 1949, du Manoir, Charles Munn and others watched the Seminole tribe parading "in their picturesque native costumes," adding "a colorful touch to the event." To add even more color, hundreds of Hialeah's pink flamingos that lived on a small island in the center of the track took flight before the clubhouse and grandstand.[152]

Joseph E. Widener was responsible for importing the famous flamingos from Cuba in the early 1930s and added more from that country and South America a few years later. His track superintendent fed them a "steady diet of shrimp and cod liver oil to bring out their gorgeous color."[153]

In 1941, du Manoir wrote a charming history of the Hialeah Park flamingos:

> *The story of their life at Hialeah is fascinating. The first batch was imported from South America many years ago and were turned loose on their new home. But these aristocrats of the winged world felt dissatisfied with the food, the service, and the surroundings. They promptly flew away to the great despair of the Management. A second batch was shipped from their native land to replace the fugitives. They were immediately treated with all the care and attention due to their high rank among the feathered species. A new, more picturesque and comfortable island was built for them. Their food was ordered "a la carte" and served at the very time that best suited their appetite. Life was rosy for our pink friends. Yet it was not perfect happiness for the Flamingo Colony. For four long years, not a single egg was laid, not a single baby flamingo was born. The hopes of the Management that they would prosper and multiply were painfully shattered. It seemed as though the days of the herd were counted.*
>
> *The flamingoes are an ultra-smart set. And like in every smart set no Flamingo wanted to do something that might not be fashionable. None of them were quite certain [if] it were or not quite the thing to do to lay an egg. So, for four years...four long years, they went on a standing up strike. No little flamingoes and the old ones dying at increasing pace from nervous breakdowns!!!*
>
> *But one good morning, Miracle of Miracles, one of the most socially prominent middle-aged hens laid an egg in full view of the whole colony.*

Vintage Miami Beach Glamour

This scandal, for a scandal it was at the time in its novelty, originated among the flamingoes the deafening "gab-gab-gab" that you still hear to this day. But the fashion was established…gab-gab-gab or no gab-gab-gab.… Today our Flamingo friends prosper and multiply and their Hialeah Paradise is filled with glee!!!!![154]

Chapter 8
HOLLYWOOD COMES TO MIAMI BEACH

From 1936 to 1937, du Manoir traveled around the world, satisfying a lust for exploration and photographing exotic places. He rode elephants in India, witnessed a snake charmer in Cairo and held a rumba class for the lovely young natives of Bali. Before du Manoir left France in February 1937, former minister of the interior Louis-Jean Malvy sent the count his best wishes for a *merveilleux* voyage.[155]

Du Manoir returned to Miami Beach by April 1937. Later that year, the Giffords moved from Alton Road to Sunset Island II, one in a group of four small, exclusive islands in Biscayne Bay just off Miami Beach. Of course, the count moved with them and in doing so, joined that social clique.[156]

The elite Sunset Islands dwellers included du Manoir's friend, Asheville, North Carolina–born movie theater pioneer Stephen Andrew Lynch (1882–1969), who had maintained a residence in Atlanta for a time. A dynamic real estate investor, Lynch was largely responsible for developing the four man-made isles, and in June 1926, his company was in the process of filling them in. Although planned to be completed by December, the devastating September hurricane and general poor economy compelled Lynch to hold onto them until 1930. In August of that year, he stated through his lawyer that "for a long time a large force of men has been at work on these islands without any publicity being given, and the project with its heavy payroll, has gone steadily ahead, regardless of general business conditions." Even during the Great Depression, Lynch's perseverance exemplified an optimistic market for luxury real estate, and by 1932, several tracts were for sale, mostly offered by Lynch's Sunset Island Company but others by the Miami Beach Bayshore Company, a Carl Fisher–controlled corporation he held with the Collins/Pancoast family.[157]

Du Manoir and the Giffords loved their Sunset Island II home and lived there for many years. In November 1948, the count was so content on the island that he wrote, "Let me have Miami Beach and I will ask for nothing more." Both the Bath Club and Surf Club had undergone remodeling that month and were scheduled to be opened by mid-December.[158]

At the end of November, Hollywood stars Richard Widmark, Linda Darnell and Miami High School alumnus Constance "Connie" Keane—better known as Veronica Lake of the famous peek-a-boo hairdo—along with handsome actor John Russell, began filming *Slattery's Hurricane* at Villa Tranquilla. A beautiful mansion on the southwestern tip of Sunset Island I, Villa Tranquilla was built by architect Maurice Fatio in 1936 for Ernest and Vera Martin. Aleda and Guilford Hall purchased the home in 1946, and thereafter, the eleven-thousand-square-foot manse, boasting a façade of quarry keystone and an elegant entranceway, was called at times by its alternative name—Guilford Hall.[159]

Directed by Veronica Lake's husband, Andre de Toth, *Slattery's Hurricane* was produced by William Perlberg for Twentieth Century Fox. Linda Darnell resented the studio for sending her to Florida to make the film instead of assigning her to play the coveted title role of *Pinky*, which instead went to Jeanne Crain, who earned an Academy Award nomination for her performance. Darnell also missed her adopted child in California and longed for her lover, Joseph Mankiewicz, who had just directed her in the triumphant *Letter to Three Wives*. Nevertheless, the twenty-five-year-old actress was comforted to see her trusted hair stylist, Gladys Witten, who welcomed Darnell in Miami Beach. Despite Darnell's low spirits, she persevered with her role, and fortunately, the entire cast was harmonious and friendly toward one another during the shoot.[160]

In the first week of filming amid tight security, police kept curious onlookers from entering Sunset Island I. However, du Manoir, who lived on the adjacent island, had good friends, such as champion runner Ray Dodge and his wife, Ada (a former actress), who lived nearby Villa Tranquilla, so the count was invited to watch the stars in action. Linda Darnell and Veronica Lake captivated him, and the latest Fox discovery, John Russell, entranced "the smart set and not a few lonely ladies, who spent hours every day admiring" him.[161]

Celebrities and Socialites in the Heyday of Chic

Villa Tranquilla, Sunset Island I, Miami Beach, built by Maurice Fatio, 1936. *Photographer unknown, courtesy the Historical Society of Palm Beach County.*

Candid photograph of Linda Darnell, Richard Widmark and Veronica Lake relaxing on the set of *Slattery's Hurricane* at Villa Tranquilla, Miami Beach, 1948. *Miami News Collection, HistoryMiami Museum, 1989-011-21820.*

Vintage Miami Beach Glamour

Veronica Lake had to burst into an emotional scene fifteen times before her husband accepted it as the ultimate take. While du Manoir enjoyed her performance, as well as those of the other actors, he questioned "the good taste of our guests from California in using the word 'hurricane' while they are enjoying the hospitality of our shores," especially since South Florida had experienced hurricanes that year. Therefore, the count retitled the movie *Slattery's Wind-blow*.[162]

Actor John Russell. *Glossy reprint, photographer unknown, author's collection.*

Throughout the approximately three-week shoot, the production company used other local settings as well, such as the Biscayne Palace restaurant/nightclub at 150 Northeast First Street in downtown Miami. Under the supervision of a U.S. Navy captain and a hurricane specialist/commander, filmmakers also worked at a World War II naval air station (NAS) at Opa-Locka—where Linda Darnell posed graciously with crew members for souvenirs of their experience.[163]

In the meantime, the studio sent to iconic Hollywood columnist Hedda Hopper comical publicity pieces emphasizing that they were indeed on location in tropical Florida. In turn, Hopper reported in December 1948, "On the first day of shooting *Slattery's Hurricane* in Florida, Linda Darnell was conked by a falling coconut, Richard Widmark was stung by a scorpion and Veronica Lake was nipped by a Portuguese man-of-war. 'All we need now,' said Andre de Toth, 'is for a real hurricane to come along.'"[164]

Richard Widmark concentrated on his fine performance, but off-camera, he managed to play tennis at a local court. He later recalled that Veronica Lake, who was a pleasure to work with, and Andre de Toth drove to the various sets in his-and-hers matching Cadillacs.[165]

Ultimately, countless Miami Beach and Miami extras and bit players got their chance at fame, and the popular stars signed autographs and granted interviews to several people, from radio broadcasters to high school students. The actors and film received favorable reviews, and *Slattery's Hurricane* was the source of pride to the navy and Miamians alike.[166]

In 1949, another Hollywood resident enchanted Miami Beach when du Manoir reported, "A little bird tells me that handsome Bill Pawley Jr., son

Celebrities and Socialites in the Heyday of Chic

Candid souvenir photograph: Linda Darnell and *Slattery's Hurricane* crew at the old NAS Opa-Locka. *Photographer unknown, author's collection.*

of the ex-ambassador to Brazil, is very serious about big…eyed Elizabeth Taylor who is visiting her [great-]uncle Howard Young in his palatial estate" on Miami Beach's aptly named Star Island. Du Manoir's "little bird" was likely Young himself, as he and the count were good friends.[167]

In February, tobacco company heir Dick (Richard Joshua) Reynolds Jr. arranged for Pawley Jr. to escort Taylor (1932–2011) to her seventeenth birthday party at the Villa Venice, and afterward, the twenty-eight-year-old Pawley Jr. and the violet-eyed beauty fell in love. Subsequently, Taylor returned to Hollywood, and they exchanged numerous passionate letters.[168]

Taylor and her mother, Sara, returned by June and stayed in Miami Beach with Pawley's wealthy parents at their Sunset Island II home. There, the couple announced their engagement to the press and Taylor showed off her diamond ring.[169]

Taylor intrigued du Manoir, who was a neighbor of the Pawleys, and around July he wrote, "Bill Pawley Jr.'s fiancée, Elizabeth Taylor, is contributing valuable publicity to Miami Beach as a year round resort. The Northern press is giving much space to her recent assertion 'that Miami Beach is as pleasant in the summer as in the winter.'"[170]

Vintage Miami Beach Glamour

Elizabeth Taylor and William "Bill" Pawley Jr., June 8, 1949, probably at his parents' house on Sunset Island II; this photograph accompanies their engagement announcement. *MBVCA Collection, HistoryMiami, P109A.*

Celebrities and Socialites in the Heyday of Chic

By September, the couple had broken the engagement, but Taylor was still in love with Pawley and continued to express that in letters to him. Newspapers explained that the studio ended the marriage, as did Pawley in a later interview, but a woman who dated a Pawley family business associate claimed that Pawley's parents stifled the romance because Taylor, with her Hollywood glamour and low-cut dresses, was not the demure, debutante-type wife they had envisioned for their son. However, correspondence between the couple and from Taylor's mother, Sara, to Pawley Jr. made public in 2011 reveal that was not the case. Sara actually broke the engagement because Pawley wanted Taylor to give up show business for marriage and Sara, whose daughter's career was taking off rapidly, would not stand for Elizabeth's retirement. So, with pressure from Sara, the relationship ended, and Pawley stayed a bachelor for several years. In 1956, he attended a barbecue along with a date that du Manoir also attended, and Pawley socialized with Prince and Princess Girolamo Rospigliosi. Pawley later married but said "it took a long time" for him to get over Liz.[171]

A beautiful but lesser-known Hollywood actress, Joyce Mathews (1919–1999), had also lived on Miami Beach's Star Island and was yet another friend of du Manoir's. He described Mathews as a genuine Florida "cracker."[172]

Du Manoir reported that Mathews was first married to a colonel from Venezuela (Juan Vincent Gomez; their marriage was annulled in 1936) and then comedian and television star Milton Berle (1908–2002), whom she wedded in 1941 and divorced in 1947. Throughout their marriage, the couple wintered in Miami Beach, where Joyce's mother enjoyed a witty repartee with Berle. For instance, during a gasoline deficit, she warmly welcomed him and said, "The gas shortage is over in Miami Beach. Milton is here."[173]

In 1949, du Manoir disclosed that Berle and Mathews planned to remarry each other on June 16, and although they were to live in Hollywood, California, they would make many return trips to Miami Beach "in search of sunshine." Unfortunately, the Berle/Mathews marriage broke up in 1950, and a year later, Mathews attempted suicide in producer Billy Rose's Ziegfeld theater apartment by slashing her wrists. She recovered, married Rose twice and divorced him two times as well.[174]

The stars continued to acquire a Miami Beach glow during the late 1940s. One moonlit evening, du Manoir dined with Frances Langford (1913–2005) and her then husband, actor Jon Hall (1915–1979). The petite Hollywood singer/actress had earned fame with her hit song "I'm in the Mood for Love," introduced in the 1935 movie *Every Night at Eight*.

Joyce Mathews and Milton Berle sign their first marriage contract, 1941. *Acme Newspictures*, author's collection.

She became a regular on Bob Hope's radio broadcasts and toured with him during his famous USO shows.[175]

Du Manoir had heard Langford sing at the Beachcomber, a nightclub at 1271 Dade Boulevard in Miami Beach that hosted the gamut of entertainers from melodic crooners to such riotous comedians as Jerry Lewis and Dean Martin. The count found Langford's vocal renditions and lively personality charming, and she especially impressed him with the fact that she and her husband flew around the nation to her various engagements in their own private plane.[176]

The Lakeland, Florida–born Langford later built the Outrigger Restaurant and Resort in Jensen Beach. She was quite generous to Florida, donating millions of dollars to the state's charities and acres of land in Martin County for public parks.[177]

According to du Manoir, Jon Hall was a descendant of Tahitian royalty with a grandmother named Princess Louina. He knew Marguerite "Mano" Mersman, born in Tahiti and the granddaughter of Otto Mersman, a founding member of Miami Beach's Bath Club. When Otto's son Scudder graduated college, his father offered him a year's vacation wherever he wanted, and Scudder chose Tahiti. He fell in love with both the island and a

Frances Langford and Jon Hall stand in front of their airplane in Lakeland, Florida, her birthplace. *State Archives of Florida.*

beautiful islander named Marguerite Riddel, also of Polynesian royal blood. Consequently, they married, and Scudder became the American consul at Papeete. Scudder's daughter Mano, whom du Manoir thought was "a great beauty," with a "strange exotic charm," visited her grandmother in Miami Beach and performed Tahitian dances on the patio of the Bath Club.[178]

Hollywood entertainment presented by top-notch touring companies came to Miami Beach when, for a brief time, artist/set designer Belle Stevers and her son Richard produced plays at the Oceanside Theater on Million Dollar Pier. The Steverses gave hope to countless drama enthusiasts who yearned for a sophisticated South Florida theatrical experience. The rustic playhouse showcased the talents of stars including Arthur Treacher, Jackie Cooper, Eddie Albert and the incomparable comedian/character actor Edward Everett Horton (1886–1970).[179]

Horton led his company in *Springtime for Henry* in February 1949. In an interview over chop suey at the Fu Manchu restaurant, Horton said that he loved Miami Beach and its clubwomen and planned to spend the rest of the winter at the Saxony Hotel.[180]

To celebrate the play's opening, Dr. and Mrs. Earl Templeton gave the cast a pre-theater party on the terrace of La Gorce Country Club. While

Left: Edward Everett Horton. *Photographer unknown, author's collection.*

Right: Glenda Farrell in *Stolen Heaven*. *William Walling for Paramount, 1938, courtesy Wikimedia Commons.*

enjoying the gathering, du Manoir noticed Horton's pretty leading lady, Glenda Farrell (1904–1971), a veteran of many Hollywood movies. She felt so chilly in her thin summer dress that Dr. Templeton suggested she have a cocktail. The actress demurred and told the doctor that she never takes a drink before a performance, but as the weather cooled, she decided to follow his orders. She was about to sip an old fashioned when Horton glared at her—as only he could—and she never touched the glass again.[181]

Springtime for Henry received excellent reviews; Miami's *Jewish Floridian* commented that the stylish "repartee sparkled," and that "Mr. Horton's gift for expressive facial contortions, reaching its peak in a scene where he holds a conversation with himself, had the spectators convulsed with laughter." It added, "Glenda Farrell, in a role made to order for the unaffected actress, ably supported Mr. Horton."[182]

Unfortunately, the following year, Belle and Richard Stevers produced only one show, which did not live up to the 1949 season. Playgoers discussed whether Miami Beach audiences could continue to sustain legitimate theater featuring Hollywood stars. Fortunately, other playhouses in the Miami metro area established during the 1950s survived for decades, including a former movie house revamped into a legitimate theater—the Coconut Grove Playhouse.[183]

Chapter 9
"BLIMPING ALONG OVER MIAMI BEACH"

Throughout his years in Miami Beach, du Manoir continued to promote aviation in all fields; in fact, he spoke at the Greater Miami Airport Association at least once.[184] He felt so at home in the air that in 1940, at the invitation of his good friend Emil Buehler, he took a ride in the famous Goodyear blimp that often sailed over Miami Beach. Buehler was a visionary aviator, philanthropist, architect and engineer and, according to du Manoir, "the greatest booster Miami Beach ever had." The former World War I German naval pilot would leave a stunning legacy—the Emil Buehler Perpetual Trust, offered to colleges and libraries throughout Florida and beyond, to build facilities and provide grants and other funding for research and development of aviation technology.[185]

Buehler, du Manoir and the rest of the gleeful group awaited their takeoff from Miami, and later the count recorded his descriptions in an article, possibly for publication in the *Gondolier*:

> *Fifteen minutes later, we were up, floating slowly and comfortably through the air, and enjoying the most beautiful spectacle you can possibly imagine. A colorful picture of the Bay and the Ocean, the waterways and the Islands, big and small, that make this work of art, Miami Beach, "The Pearl of the Tropics."*
>
> *We followed the Venetian Islands for a while, heading towards the ocean. We could see a multitude of tiny white yachts at anchor in the Bay, off the Flamingo and the Fleetwood hotels. Fast motorboats were heading*

The Goodyear blimp over Miami Beach. *Chris Hansen, Wendler collection, State Archives of Florida.*

for Government Cut on their way to the Gulf Stream, and left a long white mark on the still waters in their wake.[186]

Wafting above North Bay Road, du Manoir could see his friends' houses just before the blimp soared over the Nautilus Hotel, with its Johns and Collins islands used for villas, social events and other hotel amenities.[187] They then traversed Miami Beach and sailed lower "over the Ocean, with a complete change of scenery....The beach was crowded with happy bathers, some lying in the sand, others splashing about in the surf. As we flew by, they would wave their hand or a towel in a cordial gesture."[188]

Du Manoir continued, "As we flew towards the southern part of the beach, there was hardly an empty lot to be seen but a succession of splendid hotels raising their attractive architecture along the shore." They headed closer, and the "roar of the motors and our sudden appearance would create great confusion in the solariums. Many a small and pretty figure would jump off the cots and run for cover, while others would placidly watch the big bird and wave a friendly hand."[189]

CELEBRITIES AND SOCIALITES IN THE HEYDAY OF CHIC

Aerial view of the Nautilus Hotel, 1936. *Albertype postcard, State Archives of Florida.*

They then floated over Million Dollar Pier (torn down in the 1980s), where the famous burlesque house Minsky's once stood and where the count still saw large "Girlesque" posters depicting dancers. Next, they flew over Fisher Island, du Manoir marveling at the "palatial estate of Mr. William K. Vanderbilt…with its private harbor and hydroplane hangar."[190] As the story goes, "Willie K." traded his yacht, the *Eagle*, to Carl Fisher for a portion of the island and then purchased additional property on it. Vanderbilt called his home built by Maurice Fatio Alva Base, which is now the beautiful Fisher Island Club.[191]

Du Manoir and his fellow passengers finally headed back toward the city of Miami:

> *As we flew across the bay to the Pan American Seaplane Base, at Dinner Key, and along the Bay front, over Villa Vizcaya, the City Docks, back to the "Blimp" Base on the County Causeway, we witnessed the interesting sight of the tremendous activity of the harbor of Miami, the Gateway of the South. It was a happy group…that stepped out of the gondola, with their minds filled with the beautiful and unforgettable spectacle of Miami Beach seen from the "Blimp."*[192]

View of the winter estate of W.K. Vanderbilt, its environs and the yacht *Alva* docked at the estate, circa 1936. *Miami News Collection, HistoryMiami Museum, 1995-277-16843.*

Always taking advantage of a way to publicize both Miami Beach and the aviation industry, and pleased with his article about the adventure, du Manoir sent a version to Hugh Allen, the head of public relations at the Goodyear Tire & Rubber Company, who responded in 1940: "Thank you very much for sending us the copy of your very interesting blimp article. I am rounding it around to a number of people in our company whom I know also will be interested."[193]

Du Manoir also supported aviation by publicizing his pilot friends' accomplishments. One such pilot, Lieutenant Colonel William D. Haviland, commanding officer of the Florida Air National Guard's 159th squadron, broke a speed record in 1948 for a flight from Jacksonville to Miami at 610 miles per hour in thirty-five minutes. After announcing this in one of his columns, du Manoir went on to tell how Haviland had convinced his wife, Mary, to marry him years prior to the historic flight. He had dated her for a while, but when he asked her several times to tie the knot, she refused. Instead of giving up, he "zoomed" over her house in between their dates, apparently to let her know of his serious intentions. Finally, he "zoomed" so close to her home that a couple of roof tiles flew off. Figuring that the best way to protect her house was to marry him, she finally agreed. The happy couple had at least one child.[194]

In 1950, Haviland won a medal from Florida governor Fuller Warren for safely force-landing a defective jet in the middle of an air show. Had Haviland abandoned it to crash into a heavily populated portion of Miami, it could have caused considerable death and destruction.[195]

Chapter 10
INTRIGUING STORIES BEHIND MIAMI BEACH'S MOST BEAUTIFUL FACES

Many beautiful women, such as popular socialite Joan Gentry, were regularly seen in Miami Beach, and du Manoir appreciated them. In fact, he loved to be surrounded by young females and wrote about them in a respectful manner. He escorted so many debutantes that the Miami Beach crowd and press thought of him as an eligible bachelor, although he would remain single for years.

In 1935, a blond junior leaguer named Enid Lee Lindenberg from Nashville, Tennessee, visited Miami Beach. Called by the press "an attractive member of the resort colony at the King Cole Hotel," Lindenberg profoundly affected du Manoir. In a typewritten manuscript that year, he described her as a "most charming visitor" and "splendidly dressed in a perfectly fitting, most appropriate traveling suit; every detail of her personal appearance just right, from the top of her head to the tip of her toes."[196]

Lindenberg enjoyed the activities at the Surf Club—for instance, as a guest at a tea dance along with movie star Gary Cooper; his wife, Veronica; and actress Ilka Chase, who all arrived with club vice president Alfred Barton aboard a yacht. But unfortunately, during Lindenberg's stay, she contracted tonsillitis, and her mother insisted she return to Nashville to have the operation. This saddened du Manoir, and he expressed his morose feelings, referring to himself in the third person:

> Miss Lindenberg...followed her mother's advice, and left very suddenly the hospitable shores of sunshining Miami Beach to return home, and

CELEBRITIES AND SOCIALITES IN THE HEYDAY OF CHIC

Enid Lee Lindenberg. *Courtesy Patsey Carney Reed.*

> *entrust her precious body to the care of an expert surgeon. The news of her departing was a great shock to her countless friends and numerous admirers. Feeling more than any one else the loss of her pleasant company, desolate Vicomte Georges Le Pelley du Manoir of Paris, New York, and Miami Beach, went to the station to see her off.*[197]

As a devoted aviation proponent who would rather fly to a destination than take the train, du Manoir disdained American railroad stations, calling them "monuments to an antiquated mode of locomotion." He especially chided the city of Miami for its outmoded depot and didn't see why it couldn't be modernized, because "nature offered splendid possibilities, a beautiful setting of tropical vegetation and atmosphere, to erect an attractive station."[198] He went on, bemoaning Lindenberg's departure:

> *A work of art direct from the hands of the Gods; the most delightful vivacious, and the neatest little animal at liberty, Miss Enid Lindenberg walked into the…station,…allowed her grateful friend to carry her coat, [and] stepped up the dirty stairs into a stuffy, dusty…coach. With a big*

lump in his tonsil-less throat (St. Francis Hospital, Miami Beach, 1933), the Count bade her good-bye, and "bon voyage," went back home with a sad heart, a disagreeable feeling of helplessness, his mind wandering from Miami to Nashville, his thoughts full of precious memories. She was off!!![99]

In 1938, Enid wedded Henry Murfee Carney, a respected medical doctor, but du Manoir kept in touch with her and her husband. As for the outdated depot, by 1940, Miami's mayor was eagerly accepting proposals and plans for a new, more attractive railroad station to beautify and revitalize the heart of the city.[200]

One of the most gorgeous women in the Miami Beach social circle was fashion model Bethany Anne "Bab" (aka Babs) Beckwith. Bab was the daughter of du Manoir's friend, civic leader and dentist Dr. Jesse Holden Beckwith, who lived on Sunset Island III by 1937.[201]

In 1936, Bab Beckwith had the distinction of being crowned queen of the first Orange Bowl Parade. The event was held in downtown Miami to boost the University of Miami football team and performed prior to the annual Orange Bowl football game. At its peak, the Orange Bowl Parade would attract over 500,000 live spectators and millions more on television, but Beckwith recalled that back in 1936, "they didn't know if they could get 30,000 people to watch the parade. Ernie [Miami parks and recreation supervisor Earnie Seller] and the others were nervous." She was nervous, too, and exclaimed, "I can't get up there and ride on that float!" which was wobbly. To make matters worse, they cloaked her in "ermine—really rabbit—and red velvet, and it was hot beyond anything," but she went through with it to please her father. "We always go on. People are born to measure up and do the job. All the streets were lined with people and it was very sweet....It does give me a hoot to think that I was queen of the very first one."[202]

Bab Beckwith poses in a hat designed by Mr. John. *Photograph by Philip Olcott Stearns, from Charm Photography, Annual, 1955, 38. Courtesy Vance Lauderdale.*

CELEBRITIES AND SOCIALITES IN THE HEYDAY OF CHIC

Alexander Orr, Miami City commissioner, crowns Bab Beckwith the first queen of the Orange Bowl Parade, January 1, 1936. *Acme Photo, author's collection.*

Vintage Miami Beach Glamour

Newlyweds Winthrop Gardiner and Bab Beckwith depart a Bahamian clipper ship at the Pan Am seaplane base, Dinner Key, Miami, August 16, 1938, "on their way to join the vacation colony in Miami Beach." *Acme Newspictures, author's collection.*

Still in school, Beckwith was a John Robert Powers model and subsequently posed in countless ads for everything from soap to chewing gum. She appeared on covers of such chic magazines as *Vogue* and *Cosmopolitan*; in fact, she succeeded handily as a Powers cover girl for ten years.[203]

During her reign as a top model, Beckwith traveled to Hollywood to pursue a movie career. In 1937, Paramount signed her to a six-month contract with a five-year option, but love conquered stardom in 1938 when she married Winthrop "Winnie" Gardiner Jr., a multimillionaire scion of the prominent Gardiner's Island family from East Hampton, Long Island, New York. The couple enjoyed socializing in Miami Beach during the winter season, but sadly, they divorced in 1941.[204]

As an intelligent, cultured and enterprising divorcée, Beckwith had considerably more to offer than an exquisite, heart-shaped face. She could have captured just about any other man she desired, but her primary passion was flying. She enrolled in the Civilian Pilot Training Program at Embry-Riddle School of Aviation in Miami and earned a private pilot's license in the same year as her divorce. Her dad, Jesse, was her first passenger, but not before he "kissed a rabbit's foot," said goodbye to all his friends and insisted the plane be equipped with three parachutes. In December 1941, MGM gave Beckwith a Hollywood screen test, but producer Mervyn Leroy, while proud of his latest discovery, didn't want her to fly, so she returned to Miami to achieve loftier goals and eventually obtained commercial and instructor pilot licenses.[205]

During World War II, Beckwith served her country by teaching Miami-area U.S. Army Air Corps pilots how to properly operate a plane.[206] Around April 1944, her friend Randolph A. Hearst (who would become the father of Patricia "Patty" Hearst) introduced her to a young, handsome lieutenant named Jack Kennedy, who was stationed with the Miami PT Shakedown unit, an adjunct of the Submarine Chasing Training Center. The future president John F. Kennedy, Beckwith and Hearst went to Miami Beach's Bath Club and had a wonderful time.[207]

After the outing, Kennedy wooed Beckwith with gusto, and the two saw each other frequently. She called him "Jackson" and described him as "very cute," "easygoing" and "happy-go-lucky." They often had fun together; he "laughed all the time," and one night, they swam off the Miami Beach coast and drank chilled champagne.[208]

They were close enough for Kennedy to confide in her that he "never prayed so much" as when he almost drowned after the 1943 PT-109 collision with the Japanese destroyer *Amagiri*. However, Beckwith had been seriously dating a gentleman who perished in World War II, and she thought of Kennedy as "a darling friend, nothing more."[209]

According to another naval officer stationed in Miami, one night in Beckwith's apartment, she thought Kennedy seemed more interested in a radio broadcast than her, so she asked him to leave. However, two Kennedy biographers who interviewed the officer thought the story may well have been embellished.[210]

At the end of May, Kennedy was transferred to a Boston hospital. He and Beckwith did not stay in touch but were cordial when she later saw him at a nightclub and he introduced her to his wife, Jacqueline.[211]

In the meantime, after World War II, Beckwith volunteered for the Red Cross, transporting paraplegic veterans by bus. In 1945, she married artist Dana Gibson Noble, with whom she had a son in 1946, but unfortunately, the marriage ended in divorce.[212]

Lieutenant John Fitzgerald Kennedy, 1942. *Photograph by Frank Turgeon, John F. Kennedy Presidential Library and Museum.*

Vintage Miami Beach Glamour

A January 1948 issue of *Look* magazine published a glamorous pictorial spread featuring Beckwith in and around Miami Beach, and that March, she returned to Hollywood, employed as an executive at multimillionaire Huntington Hartford's modeling agency. Then, for about half a year from 1948 to 1949, she worked in a top-secret manner for Howard Hughes, owner of RKO, and Samuel Goldwyn, whose pictures RKO distributed. Her undercover job consisted of advising starlets on how to dress fashionably, style their hair, apply makeup and conduct themselves at dinner parties and other events in the public eye. While in Hollywood, Beckwith drove the famous Tucker automobile and concurred with Hughes that its front end was too lightweight.[213]

After she returned to Florida in 1949, Beckwith attended a Miami Beach party given by singer/composer Shirley Cowell. Du Manoir was there and noted that Bab looked "like a million dollars after six months of hard and confidential work with Howard Hughes in California" and added that she "was her usual charming self and greeted with obvious pleasure the many friends she had not seen for so long." Her date was Carl Larsen, a Detroit millionaire who often saw her between marriages.[214]

The same year, Beckwith served as a charter member of Miami's All American Fashion Pageant Committee. The pageant was a promotional event to attract an international clientele to fashion merchants along Lincoln Road and other retail clothing stores in the Greater Miami area.[215]

During the early 1950s, Beckwith maintained a warm friendship with Arthur Hays Sulzberger, publisher of the *New York Times*, who corresponded with her on several occasions. On July 2, 1952, he sent his felicitations upon hearing about her wedding to the wealthy Alfred Corning Clark Jr. after a brief courtship. However, Sulzberger's well wishes were not enough to save the marriage, as Bab divorced Clark the following year and dropped his name entirely, using either Beckwith or Noble. She later became an interior designer based in Coral Gables, volunteered for Easter Seals and, during the 1970s, occupied herself with writing a memoir.[216]

Beckwith moved to Memphis, Tennessee, to be with her son in 1998 and died there in relative obscurity in 2002. In her obituary, relatives noted her age as "21+."[217]

Yet another well-known beauty in Miami Beach was Frances Weinman Latimer Gardiner. While her marriage to William Carroll Latimer II did not last, they produced a lovely daughter, Cary, who would make a stunning debut in the mid-1950s.[218]

In 1942, Frances wed Winthrop "Winnie" Gardiner Jr. one year after he divorced Bab Beckwith. After Gardiner failed to convince Frances to move

Celebrities and Socialites in the Heyday of Chic

Frances Weinman (Latimer Gardiner Luro). *Image courtesy Robert W. Avent.*

to Latin America, they divorced in early 1949, and in September of that year, Winthrop Gardiner married world champion and Olympic gold medal ice-skating sensation/movie star Sonja Henie, the former wife of Miami Beach socialite Daniel Topping, co-owner of the New York Yankees.[219]

By then, Frances's mother, Mrs. William (Caroline) Weinman, had purchased Jane Fisher's "palatial" home at 4760 North Bay Road, and thereafter, Frances Gardiner attended several seasonal parties there. (Fisher had moved to a "little jewel" on Biscayne Island at that time.)[220]

Gardiner and du Manoir attended Surf Club events together, including one honoring actor Joseph Cotten. In 1949, the count commented that Gardiner, "Miami Beach's most charming…southern belle is in Seventh Heaven." She showed off a gold enamel bracelet with yacht signal flags spelling out "Darling" and was "madly in love again." He continued, "This time, it is definitely the real thing. Frances, who after her recent divorce from Winnie…had been planning to go farming in the fertile soil of Virginia, has changed her plans. It's bye-bye to the farm, the cows, the cornfields, and the horses. The slim red head beauty is taking up yachting as a hobby and a famous yachtsman as a hubby."[221]

Gardiner had been seen with international attorney N. Henry Josephs, who romanced her while yachting in Cannes and en route to the United States aboard a ship.[222] However, she didn't marry him and instead went back to the horses after she met Horatio Luro, a prominent Argentinean playboy/horse trainer, who handled a stable of ponies at Hialeah Park. They got better acquainted at a Hialeah social event when Luro became so entranced with Gardiner that he convinced her date to switch partners. The couple fell in love and married in 1951, and Luro went on to have a megasuccessful career, which included two Kentucky Derby winners—one named Northern Dancer, who also won the Preakness.[223]

Because Frances's father suffered from terminal cancer, she, along with Mrs. John C. (Kay) Clark, founded the Dade County Chapter of the American Cancer Society Flamingo Ball. The women selected the guest list in the summer of 1965 while at Saratoga, New York, and continued planning the event throughout the fall and beginning of the 1965–66 Miami Beach season. The beautiful ball, attended by tuxedoed men and glamorous women wearing exquisite designer gowns, was held on March 2, 1966, the eve of the Flamingo Stakes at Hialeah Park. While other Flamingo Balls had taken place in the past, such as for the Symphony Club in 1956 and St. Mary's Hospital Flamingo Ball, held at Palm Beach's Everglades Club in 1965, the March 2, 1966 Flamingo Ball was the first recurring gala at Hialeah Park for the American Cancer Society.[224]

A stunning success, the yearly Flamingo Ball attracted celebrities from around the nation, including former president Dwight D. Eisenhower and Jacqueline Kennedy. After hosting the balls for essentially the rest of her

Celebrities and Socialites in the Heyday of Chic

Frances and Horatio A. Luro at Hialeah Park Race Track, circa 1953. *Photograph by Bert Morgan, Bert Morgan Photograph Collection, HistoryMiami Museum, 2016-248-182.*

life, Frances died in 1989, and Horatio passed away in Bal Harbor at the age of ninety in 1991. In 2017, HistoryMiami Museum revived the annual Flamingo Ball as its fundraiser.[225]

Another beautiful woman du Manoir knew was the heiress Brenda Diana Duff Frazier Kelly (1921–1982), who resided primarily in New York but visited Miami often, en route to or from visiting her grandmother Lady Williams-Taylor, who lived in Nassau. At least once, Nassau real estate mogul Harold Christie flew Frazier and her nineteen-piece luggage set from Nassau to Miami in his private plane.[226]

Born in Canada, Brenda Frazier had an adolescence was rife with pressure from her mother to diet because she considered her daughter's plumpness and naturally round face unglamorous and detrimental to the teenager's popularity. After slimming down, Frazier became the most celebrated debutante of 1938 and the "glamour queen" of New York's café society—the elite group who lunched at the Colony and frequented El Morocco and the Stork Club.[227]

Magazines featured Frazier on covers, and columnists constantly gossiped about her romances and allure. Women throughout the nation emulated her

Brenda Frazier after arriving at the Miami airport on November 14, 1938. *Miami News Service, author's collection.*

pale makeup, dark red outlined lips and bouncy brunette hairstyle, and fans repeatedly mobbed her in New York as if she were a movie star.[228]

In 1941, Frazier married the beefy former football player John Simms "Shipwreck" Kelly, who "knew no fear" and could likely serve as a formidable bodyguard if need be. While they mostly wintered in Palm Beach, they also visited Miami Beach, sometimes staying at the Versailles and frequenting Hialeah Park just about every season.[229]

At twenty-one, Brenda inherited several million dollars from her prosperous father. Seven years later, du Manoir wrote that she and her husband spent much of that winter in Nassau and then chartered a plane and flew off to Haiti with Prince and Princess Radziwill, Count Guy de la Fregonniere and Countess de la Fregonniere (formerly Priscilla "Dickie" Dickerson, daughter of prominent Miami Beacher and Surf Club founding member Edward Nicoll Dickerson). There, they all rode horses to the peak of the Citadel overlooking the island.[230]

The Kellys had a daughter, but by 1952, rumors of marital discord trickled into the press, and the couple separated. Brenda's suitors that year included Russian count Vassili "Vava" Adlerberg; Palm Beach socialite Ed Sheedy; the charming New York/Palm Beach artist Constantin Alajalov; and Italian race car driver and movie producer/director Pietro Mele, whom police had to forcibly remove from her Park Avenue apartment after a 3:00 a.m. argument.[231]

Brenda and John Kelly divorced in 1956. Subsequently, she had a nervous breakdown and, while in the hospital, attempted suicide. Chronically depressed, she felt extreme pressure to stay thin and "glamorous" and suffered from anorexia and bulimia. The diet pills led to sleeping pills, and she became dependent on drugs and alcohol.[232]

In 1957, Frazier married upper-crust businessman Robert Chatfield-Taylor, but unfortunately, they separated in 1961, although they did not divorce.[233] Her later life was plagued with health issues; she became an excruciatingly thin recluse and passed away in 1982 at the age of sixty from bone cancer. In a memoir published in *Life* magazine, she expressed that "though it hurts me, I must admit it: I have never known the true meaning of love."[234]

Around March 1949, another debutante came to the count's mind when he reported that Gar Wood had acquired the Fisher Island estate once belonging to William K. Vanderbilt II. Following Vanderbilt's death in 1944, noted yachtsman and racehorse owner Edward S. Moore had purchased the compound.[235]

Du Manoir mentioned that Wood, "the speedboat king," was due to take possession of the estate on the first of May and described it, including the tennis courts. He then reminisced, "On these courts, long ago, I played tennis with a young girl, Rosemary Warburton who would make bold headlines years later following a sensational marriage to a local Southampton, L.I. doctor."[236] After typing Rosemary's full name, du Manoir had second thoughts and crossed it out.

Rosemary Warburton was the daughter of Rosamund Lancaster Warburton Vanderbilt, Willie K's second wife. A beautiful blonde with a pale, flawless complexion, Rosemary led a privileged childhood on Fisher Island and traveled luxuriously with her family on Vanderbilt's expansive yacht, *Alva*. By 1939 as a debutante, Rosemary attracted attention from the press and young men in both Miami Beach and Palm Beach.[237]

During World War II, Warburton worked as a director of the Council of the French War Relief Societies, which reportedly led to her winning the Legion of Honor. She then fell in love with Dr. William Charles Thomas Gaynor, who in 1947 divorced his wife, Primrose Whitfield Gaynor, to marry Warburton. This was rather unsettling for some of the more puritanical, well-

Vintage Miami Beach Glamour

Rosemary Warburton at the Lace Ball, Everglades Club, Palm Beach, February 6, 1939. *Acme Newspictures, author's collection.*

heeled board of directors at the Southampton, Long Island hospital where Gaynor worked. They fired him due to the scandalous publicity, but his patients issued such a social outcry over his dismissal that the board reinstated him. The couple again provoked headlines in January 1948 concerning a custody battle over four children between Gaynor and his former wife, who

Ruth Dodd (not to be confused with the professional dancer with the same name). *Photograph by Clara Anna McKinney, from* Miami News, *January 6, 1935.*

had already married William Ellsworth. The outcome of this entire drama was the reported wiping of all their names from the *Social Register*.[238]

A chairperson for the April in Paris Ball in New York and the national chairperson of the Embassy Ball, Rosemary was captured by photographers throughout the years as Mrs. Gaynor until 1957, the year they divorced. From 1958, she kept on socializing as Mrs. Hugh Chisholm and was often seen with Palm Beach's fashion icon C.Z. Guest. Sadly, Rosemary died at only fifty-three in 1974 near Paris.[239]

Beauty did not ensure happiness, and this caveat was illustrated by prominent Atlanta-born socialite Ruth Dodd, called "society's most beautiful girl." A friend of Frances Gardiner's and Joan Gentry's, Ruth frequently stayed in Miami Beach at her sister Julia Lynch's house on Sunset Island II. Julia was married to Stephen A. Lynch, the developer of the Sunset Islands, and the three enjoyed themselves aboard Lynch's yacht or at the Surf Club, where Dodd socialized with du Manoir.[240]

In 1931, while obtaining a divorce from her first husband in Reno, Dodd met former world heavyweight boxing champion Jack Dempsey, who was simultaneously freeing himself from his second wife. Dodd and Dempsey dated sporadically for a couple of years, but despite the gossip columns hinting at their engagement, they remained unattached.[241]

Following Dodd's subsequent marriage to Major George Hall, the newlyweds lived on Miami Beach's Hibiscus Island. When that relationship ended in divorce, she fell in love with her Lincoln Road heart specialist, Morris F. Wiener, and married him at the Roney Plaza in March 1949. On the first day of the honeymoon, he allegedly took back his wedding gift and injected her with a hypodermic needle filled with drugs before forcing her to pay for the hotel and hospital rooms. A shaken Dodd separated from him a few days later due to "extreme cruelty, intense and concentrated." They divorced within a month.[242]

Conversely, the lovely Virginia Sargeant Reynolds maintained a lengthy marriage with her husband, Richard S. Reynolds Jr., president of Reynolds

Metals, which manufactured Reynolds Wrap. During the winters, Reynolds, whom du Manoir called "aluminum king," and his wife divided their time between a palatial home on Collins Avenue in Miami Beach and a villa in Jamaica where, according to du Manoir, Reynolds "hunted bauxite."[243]

Another Reynolds in Miami Beach's club crowd was the previously cited tobacco heir Richard Joshua "Dick" Reynolds Jr. As Reynolds's neighbor on Sunset Island II, du Manoir often admired Dick's "beautiful" and "lively" redhead wife, Marianne.[244]

Marianne O'Brien met Dick Reynolds while she was a Warner Bros. starlet hired to entertain the crew on a warship. While courting her, Reynolds wrote letters with hundreds of dollars in cash enclosed and then paid his first wife $9 million in a divorce settlement to marry Marianne in 1946.[245]

Marianne O'Brien Reynolds, 1944. Photograph by Bruno of Hollywood, courtesy Patrick Reynolds Collection. From The Gilded Leaf: Triumph, Tragedy, and Tobacco: Three Generations of the R.J. Reynolds Family and Fortune.

In early December 1948, du Manoir reported that a joyful Sunset Island II family welcomed a baby son, "a little prince who will probably share some day, with his brother and half-brothers, the profitable control of a vast and ever-growing tobacco empire. The lucky boy was born to Dick and Mary Ann [sic] Reynolds and all the neighbors on the island are rejoicing on the happy occasion." According to du Manoir, they named the baby Patrick after Patrick County, Virginia, where Dick's father was born.[246]

In February 1949, Patrick's parents, du Manoir and other Miami Beach socialites attended a Surf Club "Bonanza Suite" cocktail party and then went on to Club Boheme in Hallandale, where comedian Joe E. Lewis entertained the crowd. Afterward, the orchestra played, and du Manoir noticed the Reynolds couple dancing: "Dick and Marianne Reynolds were in great form. They are so gay and friendly. So much in love, too. The fascinating red-haired beauty has won the heart of all the members of the social circle."[247]

Unfortunately, trouble arose five years into the marriage when, during the evenings, Marianne became tired of watching her inebriated husband

Celebrities and Socialites in the Heyday of Chic

Reynolds family, December 1948: Michael, Dick, Marianne and baby Patrick. *Courtesy Patrick Reynolds Collection. From* The Gilded Leaf: Triumph, Tragedy, and Tobacco: Three Generations of the R.J. Reynolds Family and Fortune.

aboard their yacht off Monte Carlo. As a result, she accepted infamous playboy Porfirio Rubirosa and Aly Khan's invitation to dinner. Rubirosa then pursued her throughout Europe and lured her into an affair, causing her marriage to end. Marianne later told her son, Patrick, that the affair "was the biggest mistake" of her life. As for Patrick, he ironically became a well-known anti-smoking advocate due to its cancer-causing toxins.[248]

Rubirosa had a string of romances among rich and famous women, including heiress Doris Duke and movie star Zsa Zsa Gabor, with whom he had an affair while Gabor was married to actor George Sanders. The

Latin lover was also named the correspondent in the divorce between British champion golfer Robert Sweeny and his "golden girl" wife, the former Joanne Connelley.[249]

The beautiful blond daughter of John H. "Jack" Connelley, who lived on Bay Harbor Drive in Miami Beach by the early 1950s, was one of the most famous debutantes in New York. To celebrate her 1948 coming-out triumph, *Life* magazine splashed her cool, bemused face on its cover, and her renown rivaled former glamorous "it girl" Brenda Frazier.[250]

In 1948, Connelley became engaged to Sweeny, who had previously squired the excessively wealthy Barbara Hutton to Palm Beach's Colony Hotel and the Everglades Club. However, by December of that year, the relationship between Connelley and Sweeny proved a bit rocky, with columnists debating whether they would marry at all. Some claimed the hesitation was on Sweeny's part, but it was actually the other way around. In early 1949, du Manoir disclosed that Connelley, "the season's #1 debutante" had broken her engagement to Sweeny. A few weeks later, the count revealed that she had changed her mind, "a woman's prerogative," and planned to marry Sweeny after all, in March at St. Edward's Church in Palm Beach.[251]

The eighteen-year-old glamour girl indeed married Sweeny on March 30, and the couple soon entered the winter club and party circuit in Palm Beach, living for a time in a house abutting the Everglades Club golf course. Often reported on by Miami columnists, the Sweenys visited Miami Beach and its surroundings as well. In 1950, they enjoyed Hialeah Park and returned via special train from Palm Beach in 1951 to watch opening day races along with friends Daniel Topping; his then-wife, Kay; and brothers Ned and Jock McLean.[252]

The Sweenys were blessed with two beautiful daughters, but similar to Brenda Frazier, Joanne felt the need to remain glamorously slim, perhaps because the press often snapped pictures of her next to the tall, slender style symbol C.Z. Guest. Consequently, Joanne became dependent on diet pills. She also resented her husband's absence caused by his infatuation with golf.[253]

To make her life more complicated, in 1953, Rubirosa interfered with the marriage. One might surmise that he seduced Connelley, but the playboy purported that she invited him to her hotel room and surprised him by changing into a sheer negligee. Suddenly, a maid entered and caught them together. While Rubirosa insisted that he made a hasty exit before anything sexual occurred, the maid's report to Sweeny resulted in his uncontested divorce action against Joanne, in which Sweeny retained custody of the children.[254]

Celebrities and Socialites in the Heyday of Chic

Mr. and Mrs. Robert Sweeny on a balcony, Palm Beach, 1950. *Photograph by Bert Morgan, Bert Morgan Photograph Collection, HistoryMiami Museum, 2016-248-96.*

Vintage Miami Beach Glamour

Two months later, Connelley married Jaime Ortiz-Patiño, heir to a Bolivian tin fortune, who gave her a wedding ring worth a reported $100,000, but she said he mistreated her, and a few weeks later, she escaped from him while at a Rome rehab clinic. Ortiz-Patino reported her missing, but Connelley's father assured the public from Miami Beach that she was in a safe but secret place.[255]

Sadly, in 1957, Connelley died of a heart attack resulting from alleged abuse of diet and sleeping pills. She was only twenty-seven years old. Rubirosa's womanizing continued until he crashed his Ferrari in Paris in 1965, killing him at age fifty-six.[256]

A happier outcome was in store for the already-mentioned Brownie Schrafft McLean, who captured du Manoir's attention at a Miami Beach

George Schrafft, while he waits for his impending divorce, and his bride-to-be, Mildred "Brownie" Brown, at a nightclub, June 4, 1946. *Acme Newspictures, author's collection.*

party in the late 1940s. He wrote that she was a "northern 'snowbird' of rare beauty" and "competed with success, both in looks and fashion, with every one in this usually attractive gathering."[257]

Mildred "Brownie" Brown was a former New York model signed with Harry Conover's agency. In 1944, iconic columnist Walter Winchell raved about her: "Conover the model maker is readying a dreamboat named Mildred Brown. He threatens she will make the other dazzlers fade into the background." She married candy/restaurant heir George Schrafft in the early fall of 1946, after he obtained a divorce from someone else. The newlyweds enjoyed the season in Miami Beach, and Schrafft, an avid motorboat racer, took advantage of Biscayne Bay and the Atlantic Ocean.[258]

A few years after their daughter, Victoria, was born, Brownie caught Schrafft in bed with another woman, but by then, she had met her destiny in the form of Jock McLean of the *Washington Post* family. McLean and his brother Ned often visited Miami Beach and played golf at the Indian Creek Country Club. Their mother had owned the infamous Hope diamond, but when Jock gave Brownie the chance to wear it to a fashion show, she refused because she thought it had an evil glow. She settled for a thirty-nine-carat diamond engagement ring of her own and married Jock McLean in 1953. As Brownie McLean, she became a Palm Beach society leader who sold her palatial oceanfront mansion to John and Yoko Lennon in 1980 and celebrated her 100th birthday in style at a popular Palm Beach restaurant in 2017.[259]

Chapter 11

NIGHTCLUBBING WITH THE RICH AND FAMOUS

The lovely Joan Gentry announced her engagement to Charles "Chuck" Shelden in March 1949, which kicked off a string of Miami Beach cocktail parties in their honor. Among the guests at one of them was Cuban model Marta Esther Rocafort y Altuzarra Atkins, formerly the Countess Covadonga.[260]

The celebrating continued at Joan and Chuck Shelden's small wedding ceremony followed by an extravagant reception at the Surf Club. Yankees owner Daniel Topping served as Shelden's best man, and Topping's then-wife, actress Kay Sutton, was a bridesmaid. According to du Manoir, Topping was "a popular figure at weddings—including several of his own." Indeed, Topping married six times, five of them culminating in divorce. From 1940 to 1946, his wife was the already-cited Sonja Henie, who in 1949 married Miami Beach socialite Winthrop "Winnie" Gardiner.[261]

Topping and Henie, as well as du Manoir and the rest of the winter colony, attended Miami Beach's Palm Island Latin Quarter on the same island where Al Capone, while not in prison, lived from 1928 until his death in 1947. In 1940, Lou Walters, television journalist Barbara Walters's father, opened the nightclub, where statuesque showgirls, wearing feather headdresses and strategically placed pasties and G-strings, entertained, along with singers and comedians.[262]

Du Manoir attended other nightclubs; for example, Miami Beach's Deauville Club, formerly the Palm Room of the Deauville Hotel, where one night he was among the audience with world-renowned composer

Celebrities and Socialites in the Heyday of Chic

Sonja Henie and Daniel Topping at the Palm Island Latin Quarter, Miami Beach, 1942. *Photographer unknown, author's collection.*

George Gershwin and professional dancer Irene Castle. The count also amused himself at downtown Miami's Clover Club, a cocktail lounge where the humorous pianist Woody Woodbury entertained, and Miami Beach's Mother Kelly's, known for its owner's female impersonations and Ronrico daiquiris. Such legendary entertainers as Billie Holiday sang there, but because of segregation, Holiday could not stay in Miami Beach and instead boarded at Georgette's Tea Room in the Overtown section of Miami.[263]

Du Manoir and his Miami Beach crowd also frequented the previously mentioned Club Boheme. Like several chic nightspots, along with entertainment in the front room, the Hallandale club offered illegal gambling in a separate back room. Most of the syndicate-owned gambling casinos were well known by the press, sanctioned by some politicians and, aside from sporadic raids, largely ignored by the police.[264]

At Miami's Royal Palm Club, du Manoir hosted parties and judged dance contests. This glamorous and crowded nightspot included such patrons as Damon Runyon, columnist Walter Winchell and Hollywood actor Franchot Tone. These notables and others were entertained by singers such as Tony Martin and striptease star Gypsy Rose Lee, who performed on New Year's Eve.[265]

Run by Arthur Childers, the Royal Palm Club also featured a private backroom casino. Born in Tryon, North Carolina, on February 22, 1902, Childers relocated to South Florida in 1922 and began his lucrative career as the manager of the Floridian, a Miami Beach hotel. From 1928, he secured stars including Eddie Cantor and Jack Benny, and from around 1929–30, he ran a gambling casino on the tenth floor, owned in part by Al Capone. A shrewd promoter, Childers influenced municipal laws by retaining a seat on Miami Beach's city council for several years—an advantageous position for the manager of clandestine gambling rooms.[266]

Childers's Little Palm Club on Bayshore Drive in Miami, which also offered gambling, was established around 1943. Du Manoir deemed the Little Palm Club "always…a favorite rendezvous of the social elite," and such Hollywood stars as Lana Turner and multimillionaire Huntington Hartford were photographed together there.[267]

Among the guests joining du Manoir at a 1949 Little Palm Club party was his friend Colonel Frank Clarke. Clarke had been hosting the young socialite Virginia Leigh and her mother, Mrs. Frank (Myrtle) Delaney, at his Miami Beach home, where Winston Churchill had enjoyed his stay in 1946. The colonel's son, Jim, was as charming as his father and took a special interest in Leigh.[268]

Anointed the leading glamour debutante of the 1947 social season (prior to Joanne Connelley's 1948 reign), Leigh belonged to twelve charity committees before she turned eighteen. A journalist quipped that she had "more bangs, more tulle, less shoulder straps, and more mama than any other deb." Her proud mother enthused, "Ginny is charm herself to the columnists and the little people who take pictures."[269]

Another Little Palm Club partygoer was John Hertz Jr., who told the group about seafaring adventures aboard his schooner *Tonga*, once belonging to Errol Flynn. Hertz had married the screen star Myrna Loy in June 1942 and honeymooned with her in Miami Beach, but their marriage faced turbulent problems, and they divorced in 1944. Five years later, Hertz dated Winthrop "Winnie" Gardiner's ex-wife, Bab Beckwith, while she was employed in California and also saw her in Miami Beach. This sharing of ex-spouses between socialites continued among the Miami Beach crowd.[270]

Hertz hosted endless cocktail parties on *Tonga*, and at one in particular, du Manoir saw "charming" Bab Beckwith along with several Palm Beach

Debutante Virginia Leigh, circa 1948. *International News Photo*, author's collection.

socialites, such as chic divorcée Clarice Rasmussen.[271] Rasmussen had just earned first prize for the best-dressed woman at a South Florida swanky club, and Beckwith had been voted onto a New York best-dressed list. There were so many best-dressed women contests in those days that one of du Manoir's acquaintances, "a lovely lady with a beautiful figure," tired of them and offered an alternative: "What about the best undressed women? Don't be shocked. Let the doctors submit their choice."[272]

One of the most glamorous supper clubs du Manoir and the Giffords frequented was the Brook Club in Surfside.[273] The posh club's front room hosted elegant black-tie guests enjoying a sumptuous dinner and show, while simultaneously, like other South Florida nightspots, the backroom provided gambling. Yet another nightclub with a casino that the Miami Beach circle haunted was the Sunny Isles Club, north of Surfside.[274]

At the end of the 1949 winter season, du Manoir hinted at something entirely different than in his usually light columns: "On the horizon, I find that a storm is gathering and that, in a very near future, a major scandal will burst with accumulated fury." He did not reveal the details; however, he likely forecasted a governmental investigation into South Florida illegal gambling. Indeed, in 1949, the "American Municipal Association, representing more than 10,000 cities nationwide, petitioned the federal government to combat the growing influence of organized crime." This resulted in the Special Committee on Organized Crime in Interstate Commerce, led by Senator Estes Kefauver.[275]

Raids on nightclubs had already occurred in the 1940s, but beginning in May 1950, the committee thoroughly probed all the clandestine casinos in Miami-area nightspots that du Manoir and his friends frequented, as well as numerous other restaurants and retail outlets. The commission concluded that gambling proliferated throughout the Miami metropolitan area and that the syndicate that organized the gaming was tied to politicians as prominent as the Florida governor. Many arrests ensued, as did numerous additional raids, and fines were levied against gang leaders such as Meyer Lansky, but Arthur Childers endured, as did South Florida nightlife.[276]

Chapter 12
DESTINATIONS OF MIAMI BEACH'S COLONY

"LA HABANA CUBA," NASSAU AND THE FLORIDA KEYS

Havana, Cuba, was a desirable and nearby destination for the Miami Beach upper class, and the count was no exception. Du Manoir spoke Spanish fluently, along with French, Italian and English, and because of his travels to Cuba and appreciation for Hispanic culture, he became the head of the Latin American department at the John C. Frazure real estate company in 1937.[277]

The count enjoyed visiting Havana, sometimes as a guest aboard a yacht on fishing trips or just to tour. He had many friends from Cuba, including such sugar cane barons as Julio and Jorge Sanchez, who had homes in Miami Beach, and the Fanjul family, who eventually immigrated to South Florida.[278]

Around 1940, du Manoir wrote an essay about Havana:

> *The entrance of the harbor of Havana, Cuba, seen from the boat is a most picturesque sight, it impresses on you at once that you are entering a new world. While the boat is being tied up to the dock, a swarm of young divers swim about and dive after your coins. Their cries of "Echa lo," Echa lo"…bring to your…ears the first sound of the Spanish language, "Throw it, throw it," they say.*
>
> *Cuba is an incredible mixture of the old and the new world. There is a new surprise for you at every corner, at every moment; narrow streets… will open on the wide, beautiful Avenue that embellishes the center of Havana. Rickety cars of years ago will drive alongside beautiful custom made automobiles of the very last model.*

Vintage Miami Beach Glamour

George du Manoir riding a horse in a friend's sugar cane field. *Rogers Studio, author's collection.*

Celebrities and Socialites in the Heyday of Chic

> *There are...sights by the hundred; the hat vendors, who disappear under their immense straw hats and carry around their body a carload of smaller hats and woven trinkets of every form and description; the flower shop in the open air; the...photographers who snap the pictures of the maids and soldiers and tourists in every square; the fruit vendors with their overloaded...wooden carts; the old ladies who sell lottery tickets, and the fellow who offers you, for a penny, a Lilliputian [cup] of Cuban coffee. Then, when time comes—and it will come soon and often—you will want to stop at the Florida for the famous Daiquiris. It is a good restaurant too; and so are the Cosmopolitan and the Paris. The latter is most picturesquely located on the Square of the Old Cathedral.*[279]

Other attractions du Manoir liked included the Jaimanitas Club, Nacional Casino, Country Club Park, Havana Yacht Club (where Winston Churchill would visit in 1946) and the Oriental Park Race Track. The Havana of 1940 remained wondrous to the count, but when he noticed the oversized campaign posters of presidential candidates Fulgencio Batista y Zaldívar and Dr. Ramón Grau San Martín, it reminded him of the social and political issues in a "land of great abundance, but also of great misery." Nevertheless, du Manoir had a strong affinity for Cuban customs and people and highly recommended visiting "La Habana," which attracted the Miami Beach club crowd.[280]

Another, closer destination for the social set was Nassau, with its picturesque streets and architecture, pristine beaches, clear waters and gambling opportunities. Beginning in 1934, the largest racing yachts in the world—some from Palm Beach—rivaled one another in an annual sailing competition from Miami Beach to Nassau. Another attraction for the status-minded Miami Beach circle was that European nobility and royalty lived in Nassau—for instance, the Duke of Windsor, who was governor of the Bahamas from 1940 until 1945.[281]

The count mentioned the duke and duchess in his columns because most everything about them was of interest to his readers, especially if the couple visited South Florida. And visit they did, either stopping in Miami en route to Palm Beach or for health reasons. For instance, in 1940, they made a trip to Miami, where the duchess underwent dental surgery at St. Francis Hospital. Afterward, she relaxed and recovered by touring Miami Beach and shopping on Lincoln Road and then staying at the Biltmore in Coral Gables, where the duke played a round of golf.[282]

Another important British resident of Nassau was Harold Christie, a frequent visitor to Miami Beach who established flight service between

The Duke and Duchess of Windsor during their visit to Miami in 1940. *Miami News Collection, HistoryMiami Museum, 1989-011-23730.*

Miami and Nassau. Later knighted as "Sir Harold," Christie owned several properties in the Bahamas and helped morph the area into a tourist destination. His friend and real estate partner, Sir Harry Oakes, who acquired a massive fortune from gold mining in Ontario, also purchased a large amount of land in Nassau and helped to develop it extensively. Sadly, in 1943, Christie discovered Sir Harry's body after he was violently murdered at Westbourne, his residence. Police never solved the mystery of who killed him.[283]

During du Manoir's December 1948 stay in Nassau, he remarked that the Duchess of Westminster had been visiting Sir Francis Peek and that Prince Radziwill and Count Guy de la Fregonniere (who maintained a home in Nassau) were in town "bidding bancos at the Bahama Club"—in other words, parlaying high stakes at the gambling tables. Du Manoir added that sportsman and philanthropist Anthony Drexel Duke had sailed to Nassau with Palm Beach multimillionaire Walter Gubelmann on his beautiful racing yacht *Windigo* and could not drag himself away from the lively Nassau events.[284] Du Manoir also disclosed a secret about playboy, sportsman and close chum of Errol Flynn's Frederick Joseph "Freddie" McEvoy, who was scheduled to marry a pretty Paris model named Claude Stephanie Filatre in Nassau before the New Year.[285]

Born in Australia, the car-racing, Olympic-bobsledding McEvoy had been the subject of rumors for years; for instance, he had been a so-called Nazi sympathizer who smuggled everything from guns and liquor to expensive jewels. Known as a lady killer, he married an oil heiress twice his age and then wedded Irene Wrightsman, the beautiful daughter of Palm Beach multimillionaire Charles Wrightsman, but she filed for divorce from McEvoy in 1947.[286]

According to du Manoir, while McEvoy was addressing wedding invitations, he had forgotten a little detail about his past—he was still legally married to Irene. Evidently, their divorce had not been finalized yet. To avoid a devastating scandal and possible bigamy charges, McEvoy postponed the wedding to Claude Stephanie "until the tangled situation" was cleared up. Eventually, with Errol Flynn as McEvoy's best man, McEvoy and Filatre joined in matrimony, but tragically, while on a yacht cruise off the coast of Morocco in 1951, the couple drowned in a storm. McEvoy made it to the beach but then perished when he swam back to try to rescue Claude Stephanie.[287]

The Keys were an even closer destination for a break from the social flurry of Miami Beach, and during the weekends, impromptu visits would be made. One day in Miami Beach, after bemoaning the fact that his friend, dime store heir Woolworth "Woolie" Donahue, wasn't in town, du Manoir recalled that the previous week, two other friends had invited him to Key West to meet President Harry S. Truman and play tennis with his daughter, Margaret. Excitedly, du Manoir rushed out of his office and drove his Studebaker straight to the airport.[288]

The count boarded the plane with his buddies, and while they flew over the Quarterdeck Club, the Mark C. Honeywell–built lighthouse at Boca Chita and eventually Key Largo, he kept rehearsing, "How do you do, Mr. President?" Over Marathon, one of du Manoir's pals asked him how it felt to be on his way to meet Truman.

"Oh, simply wonderful!" he exclaimed with rapture.

At that point, his friends couldn't take it anymore and burst out laughing. They had made up the entire story to get him to join them.[289]

Du Manoir called Key West a "spa for visitors in search of a short and complete rest. Except perhaps during the rare occasions when high ranking members of the government are in the town, social life is reduced to its simplest expression and so are the sources of entertainment." He added that during the spring, the "main diversion in the evening is provided by two or three cabarets where you are offered the identical spectacle of short striptease acts repeated every hour on the hour."[290] Of course, this was back in the 1940s—today, Key West offers many diversified daytime and nightlife activities.

On his way back to Miami Beach, du Manoir often stopped at the Key Largo Anglers Club, where he enjoyed socializing with the wealthy and watching luxurious yachts enter the harbor. Around the end of March 1949, he hobnobbed with professional tennis star Sarah Palfrey (1912–1996), the pro at Key West's Casa Marina. Du Manoir revealed that Palfrey would soon divorce her husband, amateur tennis champ Ellwood Cooke, and in April of that year, she did just that.[291]

The count also socialized with such avid fishermen as Frank B. Whiting, heir to one of the nation's largest paper companies. Whiting invited du Manoir to come aboard his fifty-seven-foot yacht, the *Nauti-Gal II*, and see every detail of it. Although the count commented on its luxurious accommodations, he didn't find anything naughty about it.[292]

Du Manoir returned to the Keys often to fish with other gentlemen; once, they caught sixty-four groupers and snappers near Snake Creek.[293] While he continued to enjoy all of these nearby destinations, he was always glad to return to Miami Beach.

Chapter 13
MIAMI BEACH CULTURE FOR THE RICH AND NOT SO RICH

Beginning in 1937, the Miami Beach Symphony Society sponsored orchestra concerts at the newly built Macfadden-Deauville Amphitheater at 6700 Collins Avenue. Also in that decade, Flamingo Park hosted an occasional open-air singing performance, and the Miami Beach Casino held a yearly outdoor dance festival, in which students could show off their talent. This kind of refined entertainment available for the rich and not so rich was boosted by the Miami Beach winter colony.[294]

The Miami Beach club crowd also supported culture in the city of Miami. In December 1935, du Manoir and the Giffords joined the advisory committee for the Manhattan Repertory Theater's winter season at the Miami Playhouse on Northwest North River Drive at Northwest Third Street. The following January, Palm Beach socialites made the trip to Miami for the opening night of *At Marian's* starring the play's author, legendary Broadway star Laurette Taylor.[295]

Other members of the repertory advisory committee included Alfred I. Barton; Clayton Sedgwick Cooper; Thomas J. Pancoast with his wife; and Hoosier humorist/playwright George Ade.[296] A Committee of 100 member, Ade had been enjoying winter seasons in Miami Beach since the 1920s. In response to a 1929 request from Mayor Louis F. Snedigar to broadcast Miami Beach's charms over the radio, Ade wrote back that he planned to say something like, "The man who can afford to go to Miami Beach…and remains up in the Polar regions to shovel snow and have the flu and nurse his chilblains, is simply wrong in the head."[297]

Julianne Marqua rehearsing in Miami Beach for her solo in the annual outdoor dance festival at the Miami Beach Casino. *Miami Beach News Service, author's collection.*

Along with the performing arts, many members of the Miami Beach crowd enjoyed the visual arts. As an avid lover of Hispanic culture, du Manoir promoted the art of Cuban sculptor Fernando Boada Martin (1902–1980) in Miami Beach. In 1941, the Miami Woman's Club and Cuban Tourist Commission sponsored a Boada exhibition, and du Manoir covered it in a glowing article: "Some of his most remarkable works are shown at present at the Exhibition Boada in the Miami Beach Library on Collins Avenue and 21st Street. We have spent a pleasant afternoon there admiring the talent of this great Cuban artist. We hope that you too will find an hour or so to treat your soul to a short, delightful journey to this Realm of the Art."[298]

The Miami Beach Public Library and Art Center had been exhibiting artwork since 1937, when it was reported that Miami Beach's "need for an art gallery…has been fulfilled with the recent completion of the gallery situated on the second floor of the Miami Beach Library…a focal point for the art interests of Miami Beach, drawing to exhibitions all who love and wish to study art."[299] Russell Pancoast had built the edifice, and sculptor Gustav Bohland, who believed the building would house "the finest art center and library in the South, one for which the city of Miami Beach may be proud," carved the tropical Art Deco bas-relief sculpture on the façade and in the interior of the library. This vibrant cultural center was enjoyed by all and later became the Bass Museum of Art.[300]

Du Manoir promoted Cuban photography in Miami Beach as well. He wrote an article concerning Angel de Moya, former president of Club Fotografico de Cuba, who studied in Tallahassee, Florida. De Moya came to Miami in 1949 on an international relations trip to arrange a "photographic pilgrimage" for members of his club and to display their color photography. Notable exhibitors included prizewinners Joaquin Blez Marcé (1886–1974) and Jorge B. Figueroa (1917–?).[301]

After du Manoir took de Moya on a tour through the flower-filled neighborhoods of Miami Beach, the two gentlemen lunched at the Surf

Celebrities and Socialites in the Heyday of Chic

George Ade with his pet dog in Miami Beach. *Associated Press photograph, December 9, 1942, author's collection.*

Club. De Moya, impressed with the gardens and homes he had seen, said, "No where in the world has such effort been made by the residents to create beauty and no where has the effort been rewarded with such great success. Everywhere you turn your eyes you can see a beautiful picture."[302]

Visual arts culture in Miami Beach was also enhanced by the Edward Nash Mathews family. Du Manoir was a good friend of engineer Edward Nash Mathews Sr. (known as "Nash"), a charter member of the Bath Club. In the mid-1920s, Mathews and his brother James, an early investor in Belle Isle and the Sunset Islands, partnered in a land purchase on Washington Avenue at Tenth Street.[303]

En route to Miami Beach in the fall of 1926 with his wife, Frances, Nash Mathews heard fellow railway passenger Newt Roney fretting over hurricane damage to his Roney Plaza, and as a result, Nash came up with the idea of creating a virtual fortress on the Washington Avenue property. He was sure that with his engineering ideas provided to architects Edwin Robertson and Lawrence Patterson, they could build the soundest structure in Miami Beach.[304]

Nash and his brother named the building the Washington Storage Company, and it was completed in 1927. They became exceedingly successful from the need for seasonal residents to store their items in a safe place while out of town. The spacious hurricane-proof, burglary-proof and

East elevation, Washington Storage Company, Washington Avenue at Tenth Street, Miami Beach, now the Wolfsonian–Florida International University. *Photograph by Walter Smalling Jr.; Library of Congress, Prints and Photographs Division.*

Celebrities and Socialites in the Heyday of Chic

Ned Mathews in the Washington Art Gallery, circa 1940s. *Photograph by Noel Lanham, image courtesy Pamela Mathews.*

fireproof facility with lofty ceilings held everything from sterling spoons and antique family albums to grand pianos and Lincoln Continentals. Catering to the exclusive Miami Beach crowd and beyond, the company also cleaned and treated damaged Oriental carpets and draperies. The building was so sturdy that in the 1980s, Mitchell "Micky" Wolfson Jr. purchased it to house his important collection of material culture, and by the 1990s, it had become the fascinating museum the Wolfsonian–Florida International University.[305]

In 1941, Mathews's son Edward Nash "Ned" Mathews Jr., a highly respected art dealer and restorer, took over the storage building's Washington Art Gallery, also known as the Washington Art Studio. Located on the first floor, it was directed by connoisseur and Swedish émigré Eric Carlberg.[306]

Like other Miami Beach organizations, the gallery had a Palm Beach connection. Not only did Ned exhibit the work of artists from that town, but in 1942, he and his aunt Mary Duggett Benson also founded an annex of the

Jane Peterson in her studio. *Photograph by Underwood and Underwood (who took some of the first aerial photographs of Miami Beach), Jane Peterson Papers, Archives of American Art, Smithsonian Institution.*

Conservative Jewish groups, who frequently criticized him. In December 1949, an emotional Asch spoke to a receptive audience of Miami booklovers: "I hope the time will come when my own people will realize that this that I have done is done more for the Jewish world." Sadly, by 1953, he felt so hurt by the naysayers that he relocated to London.[316]

Another artist the gallery featured was Lewis Vandercar (1913–1988), Miami's quirkiest painter/sculptor, who called himself a warlock, claimed he had ESP and placed classified ads in newspapers such as "Free cruise to Bahamas. Bring oar." Du Manoir's favorite piece by Vandercar at the show was *Modern Mother*, a surrealistic depiction of a seated nude holding a tiny infant in one hand and a gigantic cocktail in the other. The count later wrote that Vandercar, who sported a flaming red beard, shaved it and thereafter "was reported to be painting with his whiskers."[317]

In February 1949, the Washington Art Gallery held a one-woman show for the internationally renowned postimpressionist Jane Peterson (1876–1965). An honorary member of the Miami Art League and a co-founder of the Palm Beach Art League, Peterson had been coming to South Florida as early as the 1910s. During the 1949 opening reception, she "spiced up the imposing show with anecdotes of the old days in Miami Beach, when she met such early and prominent settlers as James Deering and Henry L. Doherty." International Harvester owner James Deering (1859–1925) built the palatial Villa Vizcaya, Miami's resplendent jewel still extant on Biscayne Bay; and oil magnate Henry Doherty (1870–1939) brought the Miami area back from financial ruin during the first few years of the Great Depression. He invested millions of dollars in relief for Coral Gables and purchased its Biltmore Country Club, as well as Miami Beach's Roney Plaza and the Key Largo Anglers Club. Linking them together, he formed a recreational and resort attraction called the Year Round Club, which lengthened the winter tourist season.[318]

In March 1949, Jane Peterson helped judge a yearly Artist and Models costume contest at the Surf Club with Alfred Barton and *Social Spectator* publisher Alan Howard dressed as Montmartre painters. Three years later, Peterson joined another Jane—Jane Fisher—for a joint exhibition of their works at the Washington Art Gallery.[319]

Aside from the various fine artists and famous attendees of the gallery, du Manoir made friends with many additional notables. One of them was South Florida's most renowned environmentalist.

Chapter 14
THE COUNT'S FRIENDSHIPS WITH OTHER INFLUENTIAL SOUTH FLORIDIANS

In 1940, Colonel and Mrs. Robert (Nell) Montgomery, close pals of du Manoir's, invited him to the Century Club of Coral Gables supper dance along with another friend, iconic author, feminist and environmentalist Marjory Stoneman Douglas (1890–1998).[320] Montgomery (1872–1953) helped establish one of the largest accounting firms, later known as PricewaterhouseCoopers, and founded Fairchild Tropical Botanic Garden, first opened in 1938. He named it for his friend, the aforementioned world traveler and botanist David Fairchild, who with Douglas and others helped Montgomery achieve his goal of an eighty-three-acre botanical garden.[321]

Also friendly with the Fairchilds, du Manoir often visited the lush Coral Gables garden. During festivities on the tenth anniversary in March 1948, he enjoyed picnicking on the beautiful grounds and called it "one of the most enchanting social events of the year." He noted that Montgomery; his wife, Nell; the Fairchilds; and newly elected garden president Charles H. Crandon were all there to greet hundreds of guests and supporters at the celebration, some dressed in exotic costumes. Nell Montgomery, whom du Manoir called "a human dynamo," wore a Chinese outfit as she snapped pictures and attended various booths offering books, china and other fine items. Mrs. Samuel (Isabel) Bell III, from "very much…the right side of" Philadelphia's tracks, assisted as well. Captain Thomas "Ted" Kilkenny donated to the garden Chinese and Balinese art from his worldwide travels, and with the total sales of objects and hundreds of hot dogs and other sandwiches, they raised enough money for Nell's new Fairchild Garden House.[322]

Celebrities and Socialites in the Heyday of Chic

Clipping from the *Miami News*, November 28, 1940. *From left to right*: Nell Montgomery, Douglas Felix, Mrs. Edwin Hambley, George du Manoir, Marjory Stoneman Douglas and Colonel Robert Montgomery. *GLPDM papers, author's collection.*

That year in February, du Manoir had attended Nell Montgomery's birthday celebration, held nearby in the garden at the Montgomerys' private home (now the Montgomery Botanical Center). Joining him were the Fairchilds, Marjory Stoneman Douglas, the Giffords and many other friends. In the 1950s, du Manoir yet again socialized with Douglas, as well as Florida senator/representative Claude Pepper (1900–1989), at the Surf Club.[323]

Social gatherings among the influential also took place at the Miami Beach bayside home of Baron Vladimir Kuhn von Poushental and his wife, Adele, Baroness Kuhn von Poushental. According to Adele's daughter, Louise, guests included du Manoir along with Claude Pepper and Molly and Dick Danielson. The culturally savvy Molly Danielson was a member of both Fairchild Tropical Botanic Garden and Villa Vizcaya (now known as Vizcaya Museum and Gardens).[324]

Others joining du Manoir at the baroness's house were Nancy and Bob Greene (Robert Z), a vending machine magnate. Well-known philanthropists, the Greenes gave millions of dollars to Miami charities, and Nancy was known as a leading society figure for many years.[325]

Count and Countess (Claes Eric and Eugenia) de Lewenhaupt were yet another prominent couple who visited the baron and baroness along with du Manoir. A former Swedish diplomat, Count de Lewenhaupt became the director of communication at Miami Beach's Carillon Hotel and the manager of the Barcelona Hotel and Yacht Club. He was also the president of the City of Miami People-to-People Committee. Like du Manoir, de Lewenhaupt had a sense of humor and liked to quip, "I have bread money, but I'm working for my daily caviar."[326] Du Manoir worked for his caviar as well but also relished relaxing during the holidays in Miami Beach.

Chapter 15

MIAMI BEACH HOLIDAYS WITH JANE FISHER, "SUZY," THE "TANGO QUEEN" AND AN ICE CREAM SODA

A couple of weeks before Thanksgiving in 1948, du Manoir heralded the beginning of the holiday season: "Well! I am back in Miami Beach. What a wonderful feeling to have a glimpse at the…ocean, Biscayne Bay, and the ever changing skyline of this thriving, dynamic community. To me, this is a little corner of Paradise and I would rather spend my winters here in a trailer than anywhere else in a palace."[327]

While the count appreciated his living quarters at the Giffords' Sunset Island II house—hardly a trailer—he was also thankful for his long-lasting close friendship with Jane Fisher. He shared that she had been renovating her summer house in Cornwall-on-Hudson but was back home in Miami Beach for the holidays. However, he lamented that she might have to return to the Northeast for part of the winter season. "Could you imagine Jane away from Miami Beach?" he asked incredulously.[328]

During the 1940s, Fisher hosted a radio show and wrote about Miami Beach and her ex-husband, Carl, in newspapers and the book *Fabulous Hoosier: A Story of American Achievement*. While the book was a success, the publisher of the first 1947 edition went bankrupt and had to sell the melted-down type as metal to pay off his creditors. However, in 1953, another limited run of signed books was planned.[329]

Du Manoir saw Fisher at a 1948 Christmas eggnog party, where the holiday spirit apparently affected her and Bessie Simmons, widow of prominent Miami Beach winter resident John George Simmons. After not speaking to each other for a lengthy amount of time, Jane and Bessie hugged, kissed, sobbed together and promised to be friends for life. Du Manoir also encountered Jane at yet another party in December on La Gorce Island, celebrating Cleveland Putnam's tenth wedding anniversary. The count's friend John Jacob Astor VI (whom du Manoir called "Jack") attended without his wife, "looking lonely" but happy that she was about to give birth. Unfortunately, marital differences caused them to separate shortly thereafter, and later, Astor would be involved in a major scandal with a much younger woman.[330]

There were so many parties from December through New Year's Eve—sometimes three or four in one day—that in between them, guests required naps and a couple of aspirins. Du Manoir related that the Surf Club's Christmas Eve soiree amid seven hundred of Alfred Barton's invitees was superb and also described a magnificent cocktail party and buffet supper at Tatem Wofford Jr.'s hotel. Some two hundred people arrived, including FBI chief J. Edgar Hoover and Attorney General Tom C. Clark and his wife. The count was thrilled to meet Hoover, listened intently to his recollections and also enjoyed the attorney general's scintillating conversation, as well as speaking with the vivacious Mrs. Clark.[331]

Nevertheless, du Manoir was happiest to see the "gorgeous" Miami Beach socialite Aileen Mehle (1918–2016) at the party and deemed her the most glamorous woman there. He admired her new hairstyle and personality, "full of wit and sparkle," and noticed that she had "a long, long line of handsome swains…following on her trail."[332]

The sensational Mehle got her journalistic start at the *Miami News* and later moved to New York to become the celebrated, nationally syndicated society columnist "Suzy Knickerbocker" or "Suzy."[333] However, in 1949, before Mehle's widespread fame and jet-set life, du Manoir reported that she had "gone into the coffee business and is doing very well. The most dated girl selling undated coffee!" She had arrived at yet another Miami Beach social event with one of her mesmerized boyfriends and sported "a third change of hair-do this season and a pair of beautiful bare shoulders."[334] As one can see from the 1966 Flamingo Ball photograph, Mehle continued to make an impression with her fabulous hair-dos.

Over the 1948 holidays, du Manoir's good friend and real estate boss John Frazure and his wife, Cornelia, entertained B. Joan Rentschler at their North Bay Road home. The count liked chatting with Rentschler and found her considerably interesting. Indeed, before she retired to a relatively tranquil existence in Miami Beach, she led a remarkable life in New York as a world-famous exhibition dancer, much like Irene Castle.[335]

Vintage Miami Beach Glamour

Detail, women at the Flamingo Ball in Hialeah, 1966. *From left to right*: Marquise Antoine de Rose, Aileen Mehle "Suzy Knickerbocker" and Madame Leon (Suzy) Volterra. *Photograph by Bert Morgan, Bert Morgan photographic Collection; State Archives of Florida.*

Born Bessie Morrison in the 1880s in Texas, Rentschler's stage name was Joan Sawyer. Internationally known as the "Tango Queen," in the early 1910s she introduced the hesitation waltz, brought the rumba to the United States, performed innovative versions of the foxtrot and promoted her dancing partner, Rodolfo Alfonso Raffaello Pierre Filibert Guglielmi di Valentina D'Antonguolla, better known as Rudolph Valentino of silent movie fame.[336]

Sawyer had a penchant for witty quips—for instance, a female toe dancer dances on her toes, a male toe dancer dances on someone else's.[337] Enterprising as well as talented, she campaigned for women's suffrage and was a style setter. For a time, she owned a nightclub at New York's Winter Garden called Joan Sawyer's Persian Gardens, where the elite paid homage to her chic and aristocratic demeanor.[338]

Sawyer provoked controversy when she hired an African American orchestra for her club, but her notoriety exploded when she became embroiled in a well-publicized divorce case. In 1916, attractive Chilean heiress Blanca de Saulles claimed that her husband, ex-football star John de Saulles, was having an affair with Sawyer. She denied it, but her former dancing partner, Rudolph Valentino, corroborated Blanca's testimony, as did other witnesses, including de Saulles' servants. The press elaborated seamy details of the scandal and compared the two women in photographs to determine who was the more beautiful. The

Joan Sawyer, circa 1920. *From* Broadway Brevities, *April 1921, 40*.

public ate it up, and Sawyer's alleged sexual liaison with de Saulles led to Blanca receiving her divorce.[339]

In 1917, Sawyer's name appeared in additional sensational articles resulting from Blanca de Saulles shooting and killing her philandering ex-husband. The press clamored for Sawyer's comments, but she remained silent until she wrote to the *New York World*:

Vintage Miami Beach Glamour

I am very sorry Mrs. de Saulles is in this deep trouble, and if I can help her by having my name and reputation blasted publicly I am at her service. But what is to be gained by hurting me and using me as a means to an end again is beyond my conjecture.

I find it pointless to try and vindicate myself to my friends—they all understand. My enemies will think as they choose anyway, and in a short while the general public will forget.

If the counsel for the defense will look into matters more carefully I think they will find it agreeable to save me from more unjust and unpleasant notoriety.[340]

The jury acquitted Blanca de Saulles, and ultimately, Sawyer was correct when she predicted that the public would forget, because the embarrassing publicity did not harm her career. She appeared regularly in vaudeville shows and, in 1921, danced nightly with acclaimed ballroom star Lee Tanton at New York's Beaux-Arts Supper Club. That spring, she traveled to Paris to dance in a revue and also performed in London. When she brought Paris fashions back to the United States, society women from Miami to California continued to emulate her style.[341]

In the mid-1920s, Sawyer married successful Ohio manufacturer George Adam Rentschler and retired from the theater, but not from controversy. She became involved in another divorce case in 1929—only this time, a husband blamed her for alienating his wife's affections.[342]

The Rentschlers wintered at the Nautilus Hotel by the late 1920s, moved to Palm Island by 1935 and entertained on Joan's seventy-seven-foot yacht, the *Dragoon*, docked at the Fleetwood Hotel. After the couple divorced in 1936, Joan remained in Miami Beach as a socialite and amateur champion trap and skeet shooter and resided on Sunset Island II for years. She had a bizarre habit of reporting missing jewels to the police and then finding them pinned behind a curtain or suddenly remembering she had given them to a friend.[343]

In February 1944, Rentschler wed John Gerald "Jed" Kiley at her Sunset Island II home. A detective story writer and journalist, Kiley had owned a post–World War I Paris nightclub and traveled with Ernest Hemingway. Kiley's best man was Miami Beach mayor John Hale Levi, Carl Fisher's former engineer and friend, who in early 1910 told Fisher that he should meet him in Miami instead of Jacksonville, leading to Fisher's development of Miami Beach.[344]

Celebrities and Socialites in the Heyday of Chic

Joan Sawyer and Lee Tanton dancing at the Beaux-Arts Supper Club, 1921. *From* Broadway Brevities, *April 1921, 36.*

Unfortunately, by June 1944, Joan and Jed Kiley had separated; she charged him with abusive treatment and overuse of alcohol, resulting in her fear of bodily harm. They divorced in the same year.[345]

Following du Manoir's fascinating conversations with Rentschler in 1948, he attended a New Year's Eve celebration at the Surf Club, which included dancing on the patio and life-size panda dolls as favors, courtesy of Alfred Barton. At the party, a middle-aged matron enjoyed herself like a teenager, drank glass after glass of champagne and danced nonstop. Although du Manoir did not use her name in his column about the event, she threatened him "with all the thunder of her wrath" for mentioning her behavior. Another New Year's Eve party ended problematically as well: a femme fatale teased a prominent visitor so in love with her that it drove him to a heart attack, but luckily, he recovered.[346]

After the New Year, du Manoir appreciated the quiet that lasted for two weeks until the high-season partying began. He was saddened, however, by the departure of so many beautiful debutantes who went north back to their colleges and would no longer be "bouncing on the tennis courts and diving in the pools."[347]

Around Easter, the final holiday of the season, du Manoir's friend Jacques Chevallier arrived in Miami from Guadeloupe for his first visit to the United States. Chevallier went to college with du Manoir in Paris, but their reunion would be brief because Chevallier had to fly to the City of Light the following day. After the two gentlemen had dinner, du Manoir gave his *ami* a quick tour of Miami Beach:

> *The foreign visitor was filled with admiration at the sight of practically everything....He had never seen such a spectacle. Lincoln Road, the "rue de la Paix" of the South made a great impression on him. So did the gay opening of the Chase Federal Bank, with its orchestra, refreshments, and so many flowers; the beautiful solid line of hotels; the waterfront under the moonlight; the extraordinary activity of the crowds. When I took him to his first drug store for his first ice cream soda, he watched the waitress place the two balls of ice cream in the tall glass. When she squirted the soda in, the stupefied Frenchman exclaimed: "Mon Dieu! She is putting water in my ice cream!" He agreed though, later, that it was delicious, and I had to repeat "chocolate soda with vanilla ice cream," until the poor fellow, who doesn't speak English, could memorize the miracle words that bring you the marvelous American drink.*[348]

Celebrities and Socialites in the Heyday of Chic

After Easter, many members of Miami Beach's colony would fly north and scatter to all points of the globe like wayward snowbirds. Du Manoir was no exception.

Chapter 16
THE MIAMI BEACH CLUB CROWD DURING THE OFF-SEASON

At the close of each Miami Beach season, attire became more casual—"sport shirts replaced dinner jackets"—and social activities quieted down. Nevertheless, there were still parties—for instance, on yachts to celebrate the season's ending. At one of these fêtes, thrown by automobile and real estate mogul Roy Evans on his yacht *For Evans' Sake*, du Manoir and other appreciative spectators watched an "eye-opening" fashion show, in which platinum blondes and brunettes with "gorgeous figures" modeled French bathing suits.[349]

Guests included at least one redhead—the glamorous striptease star Nevada Smith, who during the 1948–49 winter season had appeared in Minsky's Follies at the Colonial Inn in Hallandale. Smith had performed a sophisticated routine and refrained from peeling off as much clothing as other strippers. As she told a *Miami News* reporter, she strived to portray that "I can be had but it would cost you a million dollars and I'd have to be in the mood."[350] Joining Smith and the other partygoers on the yacht were the Duke of Windsor's former aide-de-camp; singer/composer Shirley Cowell; tennis star Billy Talbert and his wife; Texas millionaire philanthropist Maco Stewart and his spouse; and other socialites.[351]

During the off-season, some of the Miami Beach crowd headed to Spring Lake, New Jersey; Washington, D.C.; Philadelphia; Chicago; other Midwest cities; or New York, where they might stop en route to Europe. Du Manoir usually spent the summers in Spring Lake or New York but sometimes visited his friends in Illinois, Indiana or Lexington, Kentucky,

Nevada Smith. *From cover of* Beautify Your Figure, *a Joe Bonomo Publication, March 1946.*

where he would check out "the beautiful women and fast horses" before returning to Florida.[352]

In New York, du Manoir occasionally sent the latest social news to *Miami Herald* columnist Gwen Harrison. He reported that Miami Beachers usually lunched at the Ritz-Carlton Garden or the Colony. Some of the socialites du Manoir mentioned seeing at these upper-crust watering holes included Alfred Barton's ex-wife, the chic Cobbie Barton; and Countess Cassini, mother of Igor (Cholly Knickerbocker).[353]

At Patio Bruno on West Fifty-Fifth Street, near the St. Regis, du Manoir felt as if he had never left Florida. He saw Jane Fisher; famed sportscaster Ted Husing; Larry Smits, one of the press agents working with Steve Hannagan; and other friends. According to the count, years prior to opening Patio Bruno in New York, Bruno worked at the Embassy Club in Miami, "in the good old days when there were no night clubs in Miami Beach," and then temporarily took over the Old Forge restaurant on Forty-First Street in Miami Beach before he left and became the Surf Club's maître d'hôtel.[354]

The Old Forge was originally a studio called La Forge, where, in the 1920s, artist J. Marquette Phillips created elaborate wrought-iron gates for Miami Beach mansions. Later moving to Cuba, Phillips rescued a shark-bitten, almost drowning American cabin boy who had washed up on his property in 1948.[355] Still in business, the Old Forge is simply called The Forge and has been completely and beautifully redone.

The Giffords also had a residence in Washington, D.C., and while there, du Manoir visited his congressman, George A. Smathers, brother of Miami Beach banker and philanthropist Frank Smathers Jr., the count's good friend. Du Manoir felt "happy to walk down the marble hall of the House Office building" en route to room 102, where he saw the bold letters of Smathers's name. Unfortunately, he missed Smathers, who was on the House floor, but he had a pleasant conversation with Smathers's secretary, Juanita Thomas, a former tennis partner while she lived in Miami Beach.[356]

A luncheon at Washington, D.C.'s exclusive Sulgrave Club in 1949 included several Miami Beach socialites who got together to reminisce about the old days. The Robert Giffords chatted in a group that included James Gilman and his wife, Gladys; and Peggy Palmer, A. Mitchell Palmer's widow. The U.S. attorney general from 1919 to 1921, Palmer loved Miami Beach as a respite from his stressful position as World War I alien property custodian and continued to visit throughout the 1920s.[357] All of these notables were free from public scandal, but that didn't apply to other Miami Beach denizens.

Chapter 17
SCANDALS BRUSH THE BEACH

Scandals had penetrated Miami Beach long before the count arrived, but when it happened to his friends, it affected him deeply. A tragic scandal concerned wealthy Indian Creek Island resident and tennis and bridge aficionado Frances Lynch, who often socialized with du Manoir and took him and the Giffords on cruises aboard her yacht, *Harmony*.[358]

Du Manoir was so moved by Lynch's plight in 1942 that he saved a clipping about it in his scrapbook. Reportedly, tennis star Valerie Scott, who had lived in Lynch's house that fall, and her friend were arrested for blackmailing Lynch by threatening to publicly accuse her of narcotics abuse unless she agreed to fire her secretary/companion and replace her with the tennis player. Unfortunately, in the middle of the criminal trial, the fifty-year-old Lynch fell and succumbed to a brain hemorrhage, leaving the frustrated prosecutor without a star witness. As a result, the judge dismissed the case, and the freed Scott moved to the Midwest and continued to play tennis.[359]

In 1949, a far more publicized scandal swept Miami Beach that involved someone else in du Manoir's social circle—Gar Wood, the distinguished inventor, motorboat racer and owner of Vanderbilt's former mansion on Fisher Island. In March of that year, the sixty-eight-year-old multimillionaire threw a party for his pretty, thirty-one-year-old secretary, Violet Bellous. During the event, Wood looked worriedly at Bellous and their friend, handsome photographer Francis Howell Gardner (not to be confused with the woman Frances Gardiner), having fun.[360]

Party for Violet Bellous, March 1949. *Back*: Violet Bellous, Francis Howell Gardner and Gar Wood. *Front*: Wood's personal pilot "Cap" Weidlen and Weidlen's wife. *Acme Photo, author's collection.*

Gar Wood had been romantically involved with Bellous but at first thought she was a single woman named Violet Sanderson. However, his detective discovered that in 1947, she had reconciled with her estranged husband and had been living with him in a Miami Shores bungalow. Nevertheless, Wood continued to meet with her secretly but threatened to tell her husband about their relationship.[361]

According to Bellous, Wood had fallen so in love with her that he gave her $35,000 in bonds to divorce her husband and assured her that if she did, he would give her an additional $15,000 and a home with "no strings attached" and would support her financially for the remainder of her life. He also promised that she would "live like a queen" since Wood considered himself a king.[362]

In April 1948, Wood purchased in Bellous's name a luxurious Miami bayfront home worth $100,000, including its lot. Telling the real estate agent that he was her uncle, Wood later purported that he had merely put the house in her name "for the sake of convenience" because "he didn't want to be bothered by salesmen or the like." But when Bellous saw the deed in her name, she thought Wood was sincere, and in August of that year, she obtained a Las Vegas divorce. Wood accompanied her at the Vegas hotel but disguised himself with a moustache, calling himself "Dr. Ward."[363] Concurrently, his wife, who had a heart condition, was visiting her sister in California and died there the same month.[364]

After a time, Bellous expected to be paid the balance for divorcing her husband, but Wood refused to give her the rest of the funds, and by midsummer 1949, he still had not come through. Finally, she tired of Wood's unfulfilled promises and contacted her ex-husband for advice, which led to them remarrying in August of that year, "against the express admonitions of Wood."[365]

In October, an enraged Wood filed a $125,000 lawsuit against Bellous, causing nationwide newspaper headlines to blast their names and the Miami Beach crowd to buzz with gossip. The suit ordered her to vacate the bayfront house and surrender any claims to it, and furthermore, Wood accused her of stealing $25,000 in cash and bonds from his safe-deposit box at the Mercantile National Bank in Miami Beach.[366]

In her defense, Bellous called Wood "an Indian giver" and said he had presented her with the bonds *and* the house. By then, she had relinquished $4,000 of the municipal bonds and, with her husband, lived on a thirty-eight-foot cabin cruiser he had purchased with ten $1,000 bonds—part of the funds Bellous had allegedly stolen from Wood's safe-deposit box. When Wood's attorneys learned of this, a judge sent court-appointed receiver Louie (aka Louis) Bandel to seize the boat.[367]

The court also sent Bandel to the disputed bayfront house with an order to inventory its contents. While her husband lurked in the background, Bellous and Bandel listed the items together and afterward chatted jovially while she handed him a legally written answer to the lawsuit against her.[368]

The case went on with Wood and Bellous accusing each other of misdeeds; however, ultimately, attorneys settled the suit before a judge. Bellous returned the house to Wood, but she was entitled to keep the rest of the bonds, and the claim against her husband's cabin cruiser was dismissed. Louie Bandel earned $2,000 for his trouble and later became a respected judge, and Wood's attorneys became wealthier, thanks to his penchant for making empty promises to much younger women.[369]

Wood's timeless vigor and yen for youthful girlfriends proved profitable to his lawyers once again in 1954, when, at the age of seventy-four, his female troubles resurfaced. The year started out badly enough when his $600,000 boat, the *Venturi*, with nine people aboard, broke apart on the way from Nassau to Miami Beach. A helicopter airlifted Wood and his two young, pretty companions to safety, and other guests escaped danger in a lifeboat.

Violet Bellous and Louie Bandel smile while she offers him her attorney's answer to Gar Wood's lawsuit, November 8, 1949. *AP Wirephoto, author's collection.*

But later that year, his luck worsened when, after his keeping a twenty-three-year-old model named Lucille Stiglich in the same bayfront house where Violet Bellous had resided, the romance between the elderly Wood and the feisty Stiglich went awry.[370]

According to Stiglich, instead of marrying her as he promised, Wood had allegedly kicked and beaten her on the streets of Miami Beach. Wood denied it and claimed that Stiglich and her mother entered his house on Fisher Island, whereupon the model threatened to kill him. During the courtroom proceedings in December 1954, Wood's story seemed more plausible to the judge, who issued a restraining order for Stiglich and threw out her case. After the ruling, a much-relieved Wood and his smiling attorney posed for pictures.[371]

A few years later, Lucille Stiglich irritated another member of the Miami Beach winter colony with whom du Manoir often socialized—John Jacob Astor VI (1912–1992). Along with seeing the count at several parties, the portly co-heir to the Astor fortune had invited du Manoir to receptions at his 3115 Pinetree Drive mansion, where guests dressed formally and Astor at times entertained outrageously. At one party, for example, he reportedly hired lithe females, who created a lively, titillating scene in their underwear by wrestling each other on a wet surface.[372]

Astor and Stiglich were romantically involved during the 1950s; they had been seen together leaving his New York apartment, and their affair continued in Miami Beach. But in December 1956, after Stiglich had stayed in Astor's house for two weeks, the relationship ended abruptly in a heated argument. The distressed Stiglich left hurriedly, but when she returned to pick up the rest of her clothes, Astor refused to readmit her. In retaliation, she remained outside until the Miami Beach police, upon receiving a call from Astor, arrested her for disorderly conduct. Astor had claimed she threatened to break into his home, but Stiglich defended herself by stating that she had every right to collect her clothing and purported that Astor had spit in her face and pinned her arms behind her.[373]

After paying a fine, Stiglich was released on her own recognizance but returned to Astor's house in January 1957 and was re-arrested. Police then freed her for a second time on the promise that she would never bother Astor again, and the court delayed her trial so she could wed Ricky Capasso, a nightclub employee. Nevertheless, her new marriage and pledge to the police did not stop her from continuing to stalk Astor. In February, authorities arrested her on his property yet again and incarcerated her, but not without a struggle. According to police reports, she allegedly "stacked cots against the cell door so no one could get in, burned up mattresses, and put a toilet out of commission before finally allowing officers to get in and clean up."[374]

While in jail, Stiglich wrote a valentine to her former lover in bright red lipstick on the cell wall: "If you were with me, John Jacob Astor, the thirty days would go much faster." She was released in a few days with a suspended sentence after paying a $400 fine.[375]

Lucille Stiglich (Capasso) in her cell at the Miami Beach jail, February 12, 1957. *United Press Telephoto, author's collection.*

However, Stiglich was not quite through with the beleaguered playboy, and in June 1957, she filed suit against him in Westchester, New York, in the amount of $467,100 for breach of promise, assault and defamation of character. According to her lawsuit, he had pledged to give her $1,250 per month for being his companion and hostess and $100,000 to "postpone their marriage." Astor's attorneys thought the judge would dismiss the case because their client wasn't personally served with papers and was a Florida resident, but the judge upheld the suit, which likely ended in a settlement.[376]

As for Stiglich's other multimillionaire lover, Gar Wood, his problems with young women did not stop him from further innovations; for example, in the 1960s, he developed a commercially viable electric car. Ironically, Wood and Violet Bellous had reconciled by then, and in his declining years, she helped take care of him. According to his son, Wood revised his will in 1971 just before he died, leaving Bellous $1,000 a month for life.[377]

In 1952, du Manoir continued to deny he authored any of his columns but wrote them sporadically. Nevertheless, in the 1950s, there was plenty more to write about. For instance, a widely publicized family predicament occurred concerning the daughter of one of du Manoir's close friends.[378]

During the 1930s, the count's love of airplanes had brought him in touch with Frederick Sigrist, a British aviation pioneer. Sigrist had worked as an engineer for Sir Thomas Sopwith of "Sopwith Camel" fame during the 1910s, and by capitalizing on inventions and business savvy, Sigrist in 1920 co-founded the Hawker Aircraft Company, responsible for developing some of Britain's most cutting-edge airplanes. As a result, he became a multimillionaire who spent lengthy amounts of time in Miami Beach or Palm Beach during the winter season and owned homes in England and Nassau, where he and his wife, Beatrice, hosted the Duke and Duchess of Windsor. Du Manoir enjoyed the company of the Sigrists at the Surf Club and spent many occasions with them, not only in South Florida and Nassau but also in London.[379]

Frederick Sigrist died in 1956. Shortly thereafter, and much to the aggravation of his widow, Beatrice, and the delight of gossip columnists across the nation, the Sigrists' beautiful sixteen-year-old daughter, Fredericka, fell in love with a thirty-four-year-old New York decorator named Gregg Juarez.

George du Manoir with Frederick Sigrist and his wife, Beatrice, at the Surf Club, circa 1930s. *Photographer unknown, GLPDM papers, author's collection.*

Vintage Miami Beach Glamour

Newlyweds Fredericka "Bobo" and Gregg Juarez after landing in Miami, February 5, 1957. *United Press Telephoto, author's collection.*

To make matters trickier, Fredericka, nicknamed "Bobo," was due to inherit $10 million on her twenty-first birthday and around $25 million when she turned twenty-five.[380]

Just after Fredericka's seventeenth birthday in January 1957, Juarez asked her to marry him, and she accepted. Beatrice refused to give her consent, so the couple planned to elope without it. In retaliation, Beatrice hired detectives to follow them and prevent any wedding from taking place, but in late January 1957, Juarez and Fredericka narrowly evaded them, took off in a private plane and flew to the Dominican Republic, where they were married at a friend's home. The couple then flew to Puerto Rico for a second civil ceremony, again just steps ahead of their pursuers, and on February 5, 1957, the newlyweds emerged triumphantly after landing in Miami at Dinner Key on a Pan American Clipper "flying boat." Interviewed by the press, Fredericka said innocently, "I would like a church wedding but we did not have mother's consent. I was young and Mummy wanted to keep me at home."[381]

Fredericka's baby was due in November that year, and consequently, mother and daughter reconciled; however, the runaway romance didn't last. By April 1958, the couple had separated and battled over their daughter but subsequently shared custody.[382]

In 1962, Beatrice Sigrist married Sir Berkeley Ormerod, KBE, and became Lady Ormerod, and the following year, Fredericka wed Irish movie producer and director Kevin McClory, known for his James Bond films. One of the "beautiful people," Fredericka later married a prince, becoming Princess Fredericka Azamat Guirey, and continued in her jet-set ways until she died in 2017.[383]

Chapter 18

A FAREWELL TO THE COUNT'S MIAMI BEACH

The strip of mid-twentieth-century hotels on Collins Avenue—including the fabulous Fontainebleau, built in 1954 by Morris Lapidus, as well as his luxurious Eden Roc, completed a few years later, and Norman Giller's lovely Carillon Hotel (1958)—changed Miami Beach forever. Some of the greatest names in stardom entertained at these venues, and the resorts enticed legions of both middle-class and nouveau riche tourists, who swarmed the beach.

As development, tourists and population in Miami Beach burgeoned, private clubs held onto their restrictions, but the city itself became much less of an enclave. Conversely, the town of Palm Beach restrained the proliferation of hotel construction, enforced building height limitations, preserved several historic sites and retained a small-town yet exclusive appeal. Also, culture in Palm Beach County blossomed with the success of the Society of the Four Arts, founded in 1936; the establishment of the Norton Gallery and School of Art in 1941; and the formation of the Palm Beach Playhouse and Royal Poinciana Playhouse in the 1950s. Therefore, members of the elite circle had their own local destinations to see fine and lively arts and hobnob with celebrities and had less of a reason to frequently make the trip south to Miami Beach.[384]

In the meantime, Jane Fisher, du Manoir and the Giffords still enjoyed one another's company at private clubs and their homes. While socializing, the aging Evelyn and Bob often expressed their wishes for leaving du

Celebrities and Socialites in the Heyday of Chic

The Fontainebleau, Miami Beach, 1955. *Photograph by Gottscho-Schleisner, Library of Congress Prints and Photographs Division.*

Manoir ample funds after their death. Evelyn would repeat, "I want George to be very well recompensed at my passing because he has been such a wonderful friend."[385]

Around 1956, Evelyn suffered a stroke, and after she recovered and was ambulatory again, du Manoir doted on her and drove her around Miami Beach to see her friends. He would frequently take her to her favorite place for ice cream—Howard Johnson's, near Jane Fisher's house at 1233 Vizcaya Drive in Surfside, which was convenient for him and Evelyn to visit Fisher.[386] She noticed how kind he had been to Evelyn at the time of her disability but also that Robert Gifford began to resent du Manoir's attention to his wife. As a result, after decades of a close relationship, the men grew apart. Nevertheless, Evelyn remained very fond of du Manoir.[387]

On April 2, 1957, Evelyn wrote to her bankers: "It is my wish to revoke the trust under the deed which I made on January 8, 1938, together with amendments thereto. Will you therefore, as soon as possible, send me the necessary papers to accomplish this?"[388] Approximately three days later, Evelyn and du Manoir visited Jane Fisher and her mother and chatted with them while Evelyn stayed in their car, as she had difficulty walking into Fisher's house. Du Manoir went inside to use the telephone, whereupon Evelyn remarked happily to Fisher that she had just revoked her will because she "wanted George to have security for the rest of his life. He has been such a devoted friend to both Bob and me, and especially since my illness…and there will be about forty, fifty thousand dollars in this little trust fund, and I want George to have it."[389]

However, after Evelyn Gifford died a few weeks later, executors read her will and found that it did not include du Manoir. No such papers revoking her original trust were located, leaving no specific request as to how she would have changed it.[390]

Well aware of Evelyn's wishes for his future, du Manoir challenged the 1938 trust, calling on his close friend Fisher, as well as other witnesses, to speak on his behalf in a court deposition on May 15, 1958.[391] But even with Fisher vouching for him, the judge would not revoke the trust because of "a dearth of authority on the subject" and ruled that Evelyn Gifford's letter to her bankers was not "clear and convincing" enough. He also did not think that du Manoir's testimony or Fisher's was strong enough to warrant a revocation. Additionally, the judge felt that the count, who had everything to gain, presented "no suggestion in the record that he paid for his board or expected compensation for his services." Ultimately, by trusting Evelyn's executor and nephew more than Fisher, du Manoir and his other witnesses, the judge left him without a cent of inheritance—an endowment Evelyn wanted him to have.[392] Consequently, his future in Miami Beach was limited, although he remained somewhat of a fixture in society for a couple more years. He also continued to travel to Havana prior to the Castro regime.[393]

In 1958, another Hollywood movie filmed in Miami Beach—*A Hole in the Head* starring Frank Sinatra—with exteriors shot at the Art Deco Cardozo Hotel and swank Fontainebleau. However, du Manoir had no opportunity to see it in the making, and although he attended a few social events in the beginning of 1959, the count's life in Miami Beach would soon come to an end.[394]

That year, Robert Gifford died. By then, du Manoir had been spending more time in Palm Beach, sometimes staying with real estate developer John B. Lynch's family and others.[395]

Du Manoir announced to the press in 1960 that his yacht, the *Normandy*—eighteen and a half feet in length—had been stolen from a dock on the Venetian Causeway. That summer, he traveled to Mexico, which he found quite beautiful. So enamored with touring foreign lands, he decided to launch a new travel consultant business—not only would he plan trips for people, but he would also "accompany them on the journey."[396]

By the following year, du Manoir worked as a salesman at the Allied Specialty Corporation of Miami, a very unglamorous job. It would be his last employment in the city, for shortly thereafter, he relocated to Palm Beach. Some of his friends from Miami Beach had also recently moved to the beautiful island, and many others had resided there for years, so it was the most favorable place for business and social opportunities.[397]

While du Manoir had to leave Miami Beach because of financial reasons, he was no doubt pleased with the influx of creative Hispanic culture that has enriched Metro Miami/Dade from the mid-twentieth century onward. But as much as the count missed his former home, he continued to live, sell real estate and socialize in Palm Beach and its environs.

George du Manoir, August 5, 1960. *Photograph by Jay Spencer, George du Manoir Collection, HistoryMiami Museum, 1995-277-13298.*

While attending a party, du Manoir met up with Rieta Brabham Langhorne Westervelt and subsequently courted her. Rieta was the widow of George Conrad Westervelt, co-founder of the Boeing Company and the inventor of the NC-4—the first "flying boat" to cross the Atlantic Ocean. She and the count shared a love of aviation; both had attended the annual Aviation Ball held in Miami in the 1930s.[398]

Du Manoir married Rieta Westervelt in California in 1963, and afterward, the couple lived at her residence on Jupiter Island. They attended social affairs in Hobe Sound and Palm Beach and contributed to the Red Cross and other charities.[399]

Westervelt's daughter, Effie, was happy about her mother's marriage to du Manoir and later remembered him as charming—"a socially adept guy." In fact, she was quite fond of him and recalled that everyone else liked him as well: "He was an engaging man and knew how to get along with folks." As she explained, since high society was his life, he excelled at being a part of it.[400]

According to Martha L. Kearsley, du Manoir's stepgranddaughter, she was told whenever she acted up as a child that she must behave quietly because he had lost a lung at the Battle of Ypres in World War I. He also told Martha that years ago he had owned a Bugatti, which he loved, and that he had known the actor Douglas Fairbanks (du Manoir did not specify whether it was Sr. or Jr.). He related that when he and Fairbanks were young men about town, they rode around in du Manoir's Bugatti and one night became so drunk that they wrecked a bar together.[401]

Several of du Manoir's Miami Beach friends died in the 1960s, including Jane Fisher, who passed away in 1968. Just before her death, Fisher reportedly bemoaned how Miami Beach had grown into such a sprawling city; yet club members still strived to keep their circle insulated. By the late 1970s, aside from Frances Luro, Joan Gentry Shelden O'Neill, and a few others, many in the count's crowd had moved or faded away and a younger, more casual generation was taking their place.[402]

In robust health, du Manoir outlived his wife, who passed on in 1986. He stayed somewhat in the background of society and died in Palm Beach Gardens at the age of ninety-five in 1992.[403] Nevertheless, he left a legacy in ink. His charming observations, suave savoir faire and gleefulness of spirit, as light and airy as champagne bubbles, live on and tell the history of a vibrant, vintage and glamorous Miami Beach.

NOTES

Chapter 1

1. George Le Pelley du Manoir immigration, passport applications and naturalization records, ancestry.com.
2. Du Manoir genealogy, ancestry.com; "Wimbish Adds New Division," *Miami News*, January 18, 1953.
3. Du Manoir records; "Wimbish Adds New Division"; "Industrial Notes," *U.S. Air Services*, November 1931, 48; Helen Muir, "The Madding Crowd: Profiles in Printer's Ink," *Miami News*, December 13, 1938; "Frazure," *Miami News*, December 19, 1937.
4. Du Manoir records; "Airports," *Aeronautical Industry* 14 (1930): 13.
5. Unknown author, undated clipping (probably 1938), George Le Pelley du Manoir Papers, henceforth known as GLPDM Papers, author's collection; du Manoir, "Champagne Bubbles," XXXI, 2–3, one of a group of numerous non-chronological original typewritten articles from 1948–49, GLPDM Papers; "Miami Beach Personals," *Miami News*, January 25, 1931.
6. Unknown author, undated clipping (probably 1938), George Le Pelley du Manoir Papers, henceforth known as GLPDM Papers, author's collection; du Manoir, "Champagne Bubbles," XXXI, 2–3, one of a group of numerous non-chronological original typewritten articles from 1948–49, GLPDM Papers; "Miami Beach Personals," *Miami News*, January 25, 1931.
7. Ibid.
8. Ibid.
9. "Cocolobo Cay Outing Routs Business Care," *Miami News*, January 31, 1931; "New Ideas Said Business Need by Kettering," *Miami News*, January 28, 1931.

10. "The Committee of 100," HistoryMiami, accessed October 19, 2017, www.historymiami.org/fastspot/get-involved/committee-of-100/index.html; "Gifford Funeral Set Tomorrow," *Miami News*, July 8, 1929; "Needs of City Cited by Body," *Miami News*, December 19, 1926.

11. "Cocolobo Cay Outing"; "25 Yachts with 100 Committee, Go to Cocolobo," *Miami News*, January 30, 1931; labeled photographs, GLPDM Papers; Alfred Barton, interviewed by Polly Redford, May 18, 1967, 11, University of Florida Oral History Project, University of Florida digital collections, accessed October 23, 2017, ufdc.ufl.edu/UF00006423/00001; Universal Newspaper News Reel, "Dusky Entertainers."

12. "Cocolobo Cay Outing"; Universal Newspaper News Reel, "Dusky Entertainers"; "25 Yachts."

13. "Cocolobo Cay Outing"; "As Cocolobo Cay Club Outing for Committee of 100 Started Today," *Miami News*, January 30, 1931.

14. Du Manoir, "Champagne," XI, 1; IX, 2–3.

15. Jane Fisher, deposition on behalf of George du Manoir, in re: Trust Under Deed of Evelyn Chew Gifford, May 15, 1958, 1–3; GLPDM Papers; Judge J.P. Klein, decision, Gifford Estate, No. 2146 of 1957, 18 Pa. D. & C. 2d 769 (1959), November 6, 1959, Common Pleas Court of Philadelphia County, Pennsylvania, Leagle, accessed November 12, 2017, www.leagle.com/decision/195978718padampc2d7691644; du Manoir, "Champagne," IX, 1949, 2–3.

16. Jane Fisher, deposition on behalf of George du Manoir, in re: Trust Under Deed of Evelyn Chew Gifford, May 15, 1958, 1–3; GLPDM Papers; Judge J.P. Klein, decision, Gifford Estate, No. 2146 of 1957, 18 Pa. D. & C. 2d 769 (1959), November 6, 1959, Common Pleas Court of Philadelphia County, Pennsylvania, Leagle, accessed November 12, 2017, www.leagle.com/decision/195978718padampc2d7691644; du Manoir, "Champagne," IX, 1949, 2–3.

17. "Personals," *Miami Herald*, May 10, 1932.

18. Fisher, deposition, 2–3; du Manoir deposition, Klein, decision; Barton interview with Redford, 5–6; Effie Westervelt, du Manoir's stepdaughter, interview with author, October 11, 2017.

Chapter 2

19. Du Manoir, "Champagne," IX, 2, XXXIX, 1; Westervelt interview; Martha L. Kearsley, du Manoir's stepgranddaughter, telephone interview with author, January 30, 2017.

20. Fisher, deposition, 2–3; Jane Watts Fisher, Indiana Marriage Index, 1800–1941 (lists age as twenty-four), United States Passport application (birth date, March 29, 1885), Social Security Death Index, 1935–2014 (birth date March 29, 1885, death date December 6, 1968), ancestry.com. The birth date on Fisher's headstone

is marked March 29, 1887. Like many other women, Jane fibbed about her age, especially in her book about her ex-husband.
21. Kleinberg, *Miami Beach*, 53; Fisher, *Pacesetter*, loc. 3883–3894, 6800, Kindle.
22. Photograph by Korolden of Fisher next to her portrait, *Miami News*, August 9, 1953; "Manager Krom Again at Beach," *Miami News*, November 3, 1923; "Beach News: Social and Personal Activities," *Miami News*, March 2, 1930. The portrait's date, 1923, appears to some as 1922 with a line under it.
23. Last Will and Testament of Jane Fisher, July 21, 1967, 2, copy from Miami-Dade County Clerk's office, author's collection. In Fisher's will, the artist of the Carl G. Fisher portrait is "Wayne Adams," but it actually might have been the portraitist Wayman Adams.
24. "Social Program for Races Promises Round of Events for Distinguished Guests," *Miami Herald*, January 1, 1933; "Aviation Ball Brilliant Event at Biltmore Club," *Miami News*, December 15, 1935.
25. Du Manoir, "Miami Beach," April 20, 1935, typewritten manuscript, GLPDM Papers.
26. Muir, "Madding Crowd"; du Manoir, "Champagne," XXXIX, 1.
27. Du Manoir, "Champagne," XXXII, 2.
28. Ibid., IV, 2; V, 1A.
29. Ibid., XXIII, 2.
30. Ibid., XXV, 1–2.
31. Ibid., VII, 1.
32. Ibid., VII, 1; Kleinberg, *Miami Beach*, 117–18; Russell Pancoast, interviewed by Polly Redford, May 15, 1967, University of Florida Oral History Project, University of Florida digital collections, 9, accessed November 5, 2017, ufdc.ufl.edu/UF00006422/00001; "Bath Club Site on Ocean Bought," *Miami News*, May 14, 1927; "New Bath Club Opens Saturday on Miami Beach," *Miami News*, January 5, 1928; "Architects Sketch of New Club Bath Houses," *Miami News*, June 5, 1927; "Beach Brevities," *Miami News*, April 8, 1927.
33. Du Manoir, "Champagne," I, no. 2: 4; VII, 1.
34. Austin, *Surf Club*, 11, 18; Barton interview with Redford, 4–5, 9–10; Pancoast, interview with Redford, 9–12; "New Surf Club Organization Is Completed," *Miami News*, February 23, 1930; "Beach Building During Summer Seen Extensive," *Miami News*, April 6, 1930; Manuel Mendoza, "Surfside Celebrates Its Golden Anniversary," interview with Charles Gelatt, president of the Surf Club, *Miami News*, February 20, 1985.
35. Trumbull, *Twins' Sister*, 54–55, Kindle; Barton interview with Redford, 4–5, 9–10; Austin, "When the Beach Was Hot," *Miami New Times*, February 3, 1993, accessed January 14, 2018, www.miaminewtimes.com/news/when-the-beach-was-hot-6362394.
36. Austin, *Surf Club*, 18; Pancoast interview with Redford, 10.

37. Pancoast interview with Redford, 10; "New Surf Club"; Pollack, *Visual Art*, 268–69; Denman Fink, "Murals Add Beauty to Miami's Homes and Public Buildings," *Miami News*, February 22, 1931.

38. "Surfside Celebrates"; Alfred Ilko Barton family tree records, ancestry.com; Baker, *Jigger, Beaker and Glass*, 73; John Silva, "Social Figure Alfred Barton Dies," *Miami News*, March 17, 1980.

39. Labeled photograph of the Giffords, du Manoir and Eben at the Surf Club dated December 31, 1934, author's collection; "Smart Groups Are Present for First Surf Club Luncheon," *Miami News*, December 17, 1934.

40. Du Manoir, "Champagne," XX, 1.

41. Ibid., XXVI, 1–2, XVIII, 3; "Here for the Holidays," *Miami News*, December 14, 1946.

42. Du Manoir, "Champagne," XVI, 4; du Manoir to Gwen Harrison, "Conversation Piece," *Miami Herald*, August 23, 1950; "About," Igleheart Arboretum Botanical Garden and Bird Sanctuary, accessed April 5, 2018, igleheartgardens.com/about; Rolfes, *General Foods*, 140–41.

43. Du Manoir, "Champagne," III; Fisher, deposition, 2–3.

44. Du Manoir, "Champagne," XV, 1.

45. Ibid., "Champagne," XIV, 3; Martha Lummus, "Spicy Seasonings," *Miami News*, March 6, 1949.

46. Du Manoir, "Champagne," XII, 3p; XVII, 1; Baker, *Jigger, Beaker and Glass*; Silva, "Social Figure."

47. Du Manoir, "Champagne," ca. 1949, III; 4, IV; 3, VIII; 3; IX, 1, XXIV, 2; "Mrs. Bacon Plans Party for Veterans," *Miami News*, January 26, 1946.

48. Baker, *Jigger, Beaker and Glass*; "History," Lowe Art Museum, University of Miami, accessed November 16, 2017, www6.miami.edu/lowe/history.html.

49. Four Seasons Press Room, "Four Seasons Hotel."

50. Du Manoir, "Champagne," X, 2; Martha Lummus, "Bachelors Not Scarce, Just Hard to Snare," *Miami News*, November 30, 1952.

51. Mockler, *Maurice Fatio*, 158; du Manoir address book; Five College Archives and Manuscript Collections Series 1: Merrill-Magowan Family, Amherst College Archives and Special Collections, Amherst, Massachusetts, accessed November 15, 2017, asteria.fivecolleges.edu/findaids/amherst/ma207_list.html.

52. Du Manoir, "Champagne," X, 2.

53. Ibid., III, 1949, 3; "Bobby Jones Plays Informal Match at Indian Creek," *Miami News*, March 14, 1941; "Everett Wins Four Races in Opening Day of Regatta," *Miami News*, March 18, 1933; "Pilots to Seek New Outboard Marks Monday," *Miami News*, March 19, 1933; Trenham, "Chronicle of the Philadelphia Section."

54. Du Manoir, "Champagne," XVII, 3.

55. Ibid., XVII, 3; XXI, 2; Martha Lummus, "Kings to Combine Yule Party with House Warming," *Miami News*, December 23, 1941.

56. "Here and There, Glimpsed at Parties," *Miami Herald*, March 30, 1940.
57. Helen Rich, "From my Notebook," *Miami Herald*, March 13, 1938.
58. Du Manoir, "Champagne," XII, 1–3.
59. Kleinberg, *Miami Beach*, 28–29; Biographical History, Pancoast Family Papers 1777-1982, HistoryMiami Archives and Research Center, accessed January 1, 2018, historymiamiarchives.org/guides/?p=collections/controlcard&id=489; "Thomas J. Pancoast," obituary, *Motor Boating*, November 1941, 103.
60. "Social Coterie Attends Costume Bath Club Ball," *Miami News*, March 1, 1931.
61. Du Manoir, "Champagne," IX, 2–3.
62. "Club History," La Gorce Country Club, accessed November 1, 2017, www.lagorcecc.com/club/history; du Manoir, "Champagne," XL, 3; "La Gorce Club Names Officials," *Miami News*, February 11, 1948; "La Gorce Club Taken Over by Members," *Miami News*, May 1, 1945; Wilson McGee, "Private Group Buys La Gorce Links," *Miami News*, April 1, 1945.
63. Kleinberg and Klepser, *Miami Beach*, 91–94; "Sarazen Shoots Brilliant Golf to Capture La Gorce Open," *Miami News*, March 22, 1931; "La Gorce Lead Goes to Smith," *Miami News*, March 23, 1929; J.P. Faber, "Beach Moves Meetings from La Gorce after Racism Claims," *Miami News*, October 12, 1983; Francisco Alvarado, "A Course of Course," *Miami New Times*, September 29, 2005, accessed March 1, 2018, www.miaminewtimes.com/news/a-course-of-course-6368143.
64. "Fishermen Get Away from It All at a Club Knee-Deep in Biscayne Bay," *Life*, February 10, 1941, 43; Martha Lummus, "Social Scenes," *Miami News*, February 5, 1946.
65. Du Manoir, "Champagne," XXV, 3; Milt Sosin, "Quarterdeck Club Raid Yields No Slot Machines," *Miami News*, May 30, 1949.
66. Advertisement for 1930 annual Sunshine Fashions Show at the Roney Plaza, *Palm Beach Post*, January 26, 1930; "Experts to See Burdine Show at Roney Plaza," *Miami News*, January 30, 1933; "Roney Planning Many Events," *Miami News*, January 29, 1933; back of press photograph of the fashion show.
67. Du Manoir, "Champagne," III, 4; IV, 3; VIII, 3; IX, 1; XXIV, 2; XXVI, 3; Four Seasons Press Room, "Four Seasons Hotel."
68. Du Manoir, "Champagne," IV, 2; V, 1A.
69. Ibid.
70. Ibid., XXVIII, 2–3.
71. Ibid., XXXIX, 3–4.
72. Sertel, *Social Register*, 89, 120; Martha Lummus, "Clubs Off to Early Start," *Miami News*, December 3, 1939.

Chapter 3

73. Various photographs, writings and clippings, GLPDM Papers.

74. "France Will Be Represented in Biscayne Bay Regatta," *Miami News*, February 27, 1933; du Manoir naturalization papers, ancestry.com.
75. Label affixed to the back of photograph of du Manoir in a speedboat, author's collection; "Pilots to Seek New Outboard Marks Monday," *Miami News*, March 19, 1933.
76. "Miami Netters to Play Beach," *Miami News*, May 7, 1933.
77. "Sports Snap-Shots," *Evansville* (Indiana) *Journal*, February 2, 1933.
78. Inscribed photograph by Bert Morgan, State Archives of Florida. Some names are misspelled on the inscription.
79. "Riggs Opposes Hines Today," *Miami News*, January 12, 1938.
80. Du Manoir address book.
81. "Roney Plaza Courts," *Miami News*, January 25, 1939; du Manoir address book.
82. Warden to du Manoir, postmarked December 31, 1934.
83. Marta Barnett Andrade, Florida marriage and divorce records, ancestry.com; "Miami Netters at Birmingham," *Miami News*, June 5, 1939.
84. Everett Clay, "Sports," *Miami Herald*, May 28, 1939; "They Acquire Share of Championships," *Miami Herald*, October 30, 1949. Contrary to some reports, Barnett did not win the women's national singles tennis championship at Forest Hills in 1939; Alice Marble took that prize.
85. Du Manoir, "Champagne," III, 2–3; "Gonzalez, Malloy in Second Round," *Miami News*, July 6, 1949.
86. Du Manoir, "Champagne," III, 2–3; "William J. Tully," *Journal News* (Pelham, New York), obituary, accessed March 27, 2018, obits.lohud.com/obituaries/lohud/obituary.aspx?pid=180753831.
87. Du Manoir, "Champagne," XVIII, 3–4.
88. Du Manoir, "What About Going Hunting?" 1, typewritten manuscript, GLPDM Papers.
89. Ibid.
90. Ibid., 1–2.
91. Ibid., 2.
92. Ibid., 3.

Chapter 4

93. Classified advertisements, *Aero Digest*, January 1934, 69, July 1934, 69.
94. Du Manoir, "Miami Beach," April 20, 1935, GLPDM Papers; labeled photo of the du Ponts, author's collection.
95. Ibid.
96. "Mrs. DuPont Named to Aircraft Board," *Omaha World-Herald*, October 3, 1943; "E Paul du Pont, 51, Businessman, Air Inventor," *Virginian Pilot* (Norfolk), March 11, 1963.

97. "Richard du Pont and Helena Allaire Crozer Marry This Morning at Trinity Episcopal Church," *Miami News*, March 19, 1934.
98. Rafael R. Garcia, "The First International Sky Train Flight," *Airpost Journal*, June 1935, 3–5.
99. Ibid.; du Manoir, "Miami Beach," April 20, 1935.
100. "Social and Personal," *Lexington (Kentucky) Leader*, March 18, 1935; "Millers Entertain at Smart Lunch at the Surf Club," *Miami News*, February 8, 1934; "Crozer-DuManior [sic] Win Net Tourney," *Miami News*, February 27, 1939; "Two Miami Teams Play for Title," *Miami News*, March 17, 1935.
101. Du Manoir, "Miami Beach," April 20, 1935.
102. Ibid.
103. Du Manoir address book; "Septuagenarian Honored," *Miami News*, March 5, 1941.
104. "Mrs. DuPont Named to Aircraft Board"; "Allaire Crozer DuPont," obituary, *News Journal* (Wilmington, DE), January 8, 2006, Delawareonline.com, accessed February 1, 2018, www.legacy.com/obituaries/delawareonline/obituary.aspx?n=allaire-dupont&pid=145755168; "Allaire du Pont: A Life Dedicated to Land, Animals," *Cecil Whig* [Elkton, MD], Cecildaily.com, November 44, 2005, accessed February 1, 2018, www.cecildaily.com/news/allaire-dupont-a-life-dedicated-to-land-animals-county-matriarch/article_749c8309-1d31-51b8-884e-79a2956483b0.html.
105. Klepser, *Lost Miami Beach*, 75.
106. Du Manoir, "Champagne," XL, 2.
107. Ibid., XXX, 3; "Elizabeth Willis, 67, Patron and Composer," *New York Times*, October 20, 1989; "Film Campaign Composer Elizabeth Willis Dies," *Washington Post*, October 23, 1989.
108. Du Manoir, "Champagne," IX, 1–2; XXXV, 2; Farrell and Kellow, *Can't Help Singing*, 66; Murrell, *Miami*, 36.
109. Du Manoir, "Champagne," IX, 1–2; IV, 2; Farrell and Kellow, *Can't Help Singing*, 66.
110. Barbara Ross, "Model's $25 Million Estate Languishes While Relatives Battle Lover-Adoption Hurdle in Manhattan Court," *New York Daily News*, August 20, 2015, accessed November 29, 2017, www.nydailynews.com/new-york/nyc-model-family-touch-25m-estate-due-adoption-article-1.2332181.
111. Du Manoir, "Champagne," IX, 1–2.
112. Ibid., IX, 1–2; XXXV, 2; Farrell and Kellow, *Can't Help Singing*, 67; Kaiser, *Gay Metropolis*, 95; Herb Rau, "Raund Town," *Miami News*, February 19, 1950.
113. Farrell and Kellow, *Can't Help Singing*, 67.
114. Ibid.
115. Ibid.

Chapter 5

116. Klepser, *Lost Miami Beach*, 115–16, 121, 122, 132; Joe Veccione, "Sound of Progress Harsh at Flamingo," *Miami News*, January 12, 1960.
117. Du Manoir, "The Versailles," 1941, typewritten manuscript probably published in the *Gondolier*, 1; "Socially Speaking," *Miami Herald*, December 30, 1940.
118. Du Manoir, "Versailles."
119. Ibid.
120. Ibid.; "Cinema Stars Noted at Dinner," *Miami News*, February 12, 1941.
121. Du Manoir, "Versailles."
122. Francisco Alvarado, "Faena Lands Demolition OK for Versailles Lobby," The Real Deal, March 9, 2016, accessed January 9, 2018, therealdeal.com/miami/2016/03/09/knock-knock-faena-lands-demolition-ok-for-versailles-lobby; "Faena Versailles Classic," Miami Condo Investments, PDF, accessed January 9, 2018, www.miamicondoinvestments.com/wp-content/uploads/2015/09/faena-versailles-classic-condos-brochure.pdf.
123. Photographs of a French nightclub during the occupation, GLPDM Papers; "Gull-Wing," "Seaplane Base News," *Embry-Riddle Fly Paper*, January 8, 1942; du Manoir draft registration, February 16, 1942, ancestry.com.
124. Kleinberg, *Miami Beach*, 141–44; Barton interview with Redford; Walters, *Audition*, 51.
125. Kleinberg, *Miami Beach*, 141–44; du Manoir, "Humane Society," 1941, GLPDM Papers.
126. "Patriotic Motif Predominates at Everglades New Year Dance," *Palm Beach Post*, January 1, 1944.

Chapter 6

127. Du Manoir, "Champagne," IX, 1.
128. Gilbert, *Churchill*, 752.
129. Statement from cook is printed on reverse of dining room press photograph; James A. Hodges, "Last Minute Preparations for Churchill Made at Col. Clarke's Beach Home," *Miami News*, January 15, 1946.
130. British Movietone, "Mr. Churchill in Miami."
131. "Churchill to Paint Landscape of Miami," *Miami News*, January 18, 1946, reports that Churchill visited Parrot Jungle on January 17.
132. "Sarah Churchill to Join Parents," *Miami News*, February 4, 1946; Milt Sosin, "Churchill Receives U. of Miami Degree," *Miami News*, February 26, 1946.
133. "Mrs. Churchill Is Guest at Afternoon Cabana Party," *Miami News*, January 21, 1946.

Notes to Pages 64–72

134. Churchill to Clarke, March 28, 1948, letter sold at Christies, Lot 21, Sale 24456, *Fine Printed Books and Manuscripts*, June 23, 2011 New York.
135. Dorothy Raymer, "Showtime," *Miami News*, March 13, 1946.
136. Soames, *Clementine Churchill*, 440–41; Mabel Frampton, "Fans at Show Arrange Bouquets for Churchills," *Miami News*, February 18, 1946.
137. "Macaws Fly Off While Posing in Churchill Photo," *Miami News*, March 1, 1946.
138. "Churchill Off: From Miami to Washington," *Miami News*, March 2, 1946. Churchill was knighted by Queen Elizabeth II in 1953.
139. Du Manoir, "Champagne," XXIV (ca. January 1949), 1; *Life*, "Impeccable Blandford," 47.
140. Du Manoir, "Champagne," XXIV (ca. January 1949), 1; *Life*, "Impeccable Blandford," 47.
141. Du Manoir, "Champagne," XXIV, 1.

Chapter 7

142. Frank Ortell, "Paddock Pickups," *Miami News*, January 27, 1948.
143. Du Manoir, "Hialeah Luncheon," 1941, typewritten manuscript, GLPDM Papers.
144. Ibid.
145. Ibid.
146. Ibid.; Kleinberg, *Miami Beach*, 101, 121–22; Etna M. Kelley, "Steve Hannagan Gives First Place to the Camera in Publicity," *Popular Photography*, June 1944, 33–34; Barton interview with Redford, 14.
147. "Mr. and Mrs. Harold Spaulding Give Smart Cocktail Party Aboard Yacht," *Miami News*, February 17, 1934; "Two Hosts Give Cocktail Party for Large Group," *Miami News*, February 2, 1936; "Bonnie Scotland Is Theme at Dance at Surf Club," *Miami News*, March 8, 1936; labeled photograph of Runyon and wife, author's collection.
148. Marian Park, "Talk of the Town," *Miami News*, April 2, 1940; Mary Marley, "About People," *Miami News*, February 26, 1950; "Countess Is Guest at the Surf Club," *Miami News*, February 17, 1935; Marjorie Daw, "The Social See-saw," *Miami News*, February 8, 1937.
149. Du Manoir, "Champagne," XXVII, 3; address book.
150. Du Manoir, "Champagne," VII, 2–3; "Dorelis Divorce Ruling Is Awaited," *Palm Beach Post*, July 30, 1947.
151. Du Manoir, "Champagne," XIII, 2; XIV, 2 (repeated in XIII, 3).
152. Ibid., XVI, 1, XXIV, 1.
153. Ibid., XXIV 1; *Life*, "Natural History: Hialeah Race Track Flamingos," 72–73.
154. Du Manoir, "Hialeah Luncheon," 3–5.

Chapter 8

155. "Personals," *Miami News*, April 13, 1937; Muir, "Profiles"; Louis Jean Malvy to du Manoir, February 1937, GLPDM Papers.
156. "Personal Mention," *Miami Herald*, November 2, 1937.
157. "Stephen Andrew Lynch," birth, death records, 1922 passport application, ancestry.com; "Stephen A. Lynch," obituary, October 6, 1969, *Miami News*, Durham (NC) *Morning Herald*; "No Surprise Here at Lynch Divorce," (Raleigh, NC) *Observer*, December 17, 1924; Redford, *Billion-Dollar Sandbar*, 166; W. "Pete" Chase (sales manager for Fisher), interviewed by Redford, October 1971, 9, University of Florida Digital Collections, accessed April 2, 2018 ufdc.ufl.edu/UF00025921/00001; Kleinberg, *Miami Beach*, 94; Fisher, *Pacesetter*, loc. 3883; Ballinger, *Miami Millions*, 74; "Sunset Islands Are Developed on New Policy," *Miami News*, June 27, 1926; "Sunset Islands Project Stirs Keen Interest," *Miami News*, August 24, 1930; numerous classified listings of lots for sale in several editions of July's *Miami News*, 1932.
158. Du Manoir, "Champagne Cocktail," November 28, 1948.
159. Du Manoir, "Champagne Bubbles," December 1948, XXXIX, 2; Milt Sosin, "Film Players Start Shooting Beach Scene," *Miami News*, November 28, 1948; William H. Bischoff, "Home Town Girl Makes Good," *Miami News*, December 12, 1948; Mockler, *Maurice Fatio*, 192–94.
160. Davis, *Hollywood Beauty*, 114–15; Holston, *Richard Widmark*, 112.
161. Du Manoir, "Champagne," XXXIX, 2; Sosin, "Film Players Start Shooting Beach Scene."
162. Du Manoir, "Champagne," XXXIX, 2; Sosin, "Film Players Start Shooting Beach Scene"; Bischoff, "Home Town Girl."
163. Davis, *Hollywood Beauty*, 114; *Slattery's Hurricane* film footage, revealing the Biscayne Palace menu just before the Darnell/Widmark nightclub scene; Sosin, "Film Players Start Shooting Beach Scene," corroborates this location, also called Master Field in Beck, *Aircraft-Spotter's Film*, 177.
164. Hedda Hopper, "Friendly Florida, Falling Coconuts and Scorpions," *Evansville* (IN) *Courier*, December 8, 1948.
165. Sosin, "Film Players Start Shooting Beach Scene"; Lenburg, *Peekaboo*, 204–5; Holston, *Richard Widmark*, 112.
166. Sosin, "Film Players Start Shooting Beach Scene"; du Manoir, "Champagne," XXXIX, 2. Cast members gave interviews at the Opa-Locka airport, where the Florida hurricane hunters were stationed.
167. Du Manoir, "Champagne," XIX, 2.
168. Carrozza, *William D. Pawley*, 170.
169. Ibid.
170. Du Manoir, "Champagne," III, 3.

171. Carrozza, *William D. Pawley*, 171; Pawley collection of letters, Elizabeth Taylor to Pawley, Sara Taylor to Pauley, R&R Auctions, May 2011, Catalogue 371, accessed October 25, 2017, www.rrauction.com/PastAuctionItem/3234567; Bobby Livingston, auctioneer of the letters he purchased from William Pawley Jr., in Luisa Yanez, "Elizabeth Taylor's Love Letters to Her Miami Beach Fiancé 62 Years Ago on the Auction Block," *Miami Herald*, posted on May 4, 2011, accessed October 25, 2011, www.miami.com/miami-news/elizabeth-taylors-love-letters-to-her-miami-beach-fiance-62-years-ago-on-the-auction-block-7501; "Bill Pawley Returneth," *Miami News*, September 24, 1956.
172. Du Manoir, "Champagne," III, 3–4.
173. Ibid., III, 3–4; Milt Sosin, "Milton Berle to Rewed Joyce Mathews of Beach," *Miami News*, June 2, 1949.
174. Du Manoir, "Champagne," III, 1949, 4; labeled press photograph of Mathews, with injured wrists, entering the hospital, July 15, 1951.
175. Du Manoir, "Champagne," XXX, 1–2.
176. Ibid.
177. Wright, *More than Petticoats*, 136–42.
178. Du Manoir, "Champagne," XXX, 1–2; Nichole Fuller, Marguerite Borntraeger Jamison obituary, *Pittsburgh Post-Gazette*, March 31, 2005.
179. Du Manoir, "Champagne," XVIII, 4–5; "Miami Theater Opens Feb. 1," *Billboard*, January 22, 1949.
180. Connie Gee, "'Henry' Considers Clubwomen Fine," *Miami News*, February 1, 1949.
181. Du Manoir, "Champagne," XXIII, 2.
182. "Horton Receives Praise from Performance Here," *Jewish Floridian*, February 4, 1949.
183. Herb Rau, "Raund Town," *Miami News*, March 21, 1950.

Chapter 9

184. "Du Manoir to Talk," *Miami News*, May 11, 1937.
185. Du Manoir, "Blimping Along Over Miami Beach," 1940, 1–2, GLPDM Papers; Bergen Community College, "About Emil Buehler," accessed December 21, 2018, bergen.edu/academics/academic-divisions-departments/computer-science-information-engineering-technologies/aviation-program/about-emil-buehler.
186. Du Manoir, "Blimping," 1.
187. Klepser, *Lost Miami Beach*, 116.
188. Du Manoir, "Blimping," 1–2.
189. Ibid.
190. Ibid., 2–3.

191. Fisher, *Pacesetter*, loc. 5723; Gittelman, *Willie K. Vanderbilt II*, 190.
192. Du Manoir, "Blimping," 3.
193. Allen to Manoir, April 10, 1940, GLPDM papers.
194. Du Manoir, "Champagne," XXXIX, 3–4.
195. "Col. Haviland Gets Air Medal," *Palm Beach Post*, September 20, 1950.

Chapter 10

196. "Junior Leaguer," *Miami News*, March 16, 1935; "Smart Tea Dance Given by Visitors at the Surf Club," *Miami News*, March 8, 1935; du Manoir, typewritten manuscript, "Miami Beach, Florida, March 10 Associated Press," GLPDM Papers.
197. Du Manoir, "Miami Beach"; "Smart Tea Dance Given."
198. Du Manoir, "Miami Beach."
199. Ibid.
200. Du Manoir, address book; "About the Station," *Miami News*, September 1, 1940.
201. Labeled press photograph of Bab as first Orange Bowl queen, 1936; Edith Robertson, "Bab Was the Beauty in the First Parade," *Miami News*, January 1, 1977; du Manoir, address book.
202. Robertson, "Bab Was the Beauty."
203. Jerry Mason, "This Glamour Girl, a Pilot, Is Teaching Soldiers How to Fly," *Boston Herald*, March 26, 1944.
204. "The Boulevardiere," *Miami News*, March 17, 1937; labeled photograph of newlyweds Gardiner and Beckwith, August 16, 1938; Gardiner/Beckwith marriage and divorce records, ancestry.com; Leonard Lyons, "The Lyon's Den," *Miami News*, December 9, 1941;
205. Mason, "Glamour Girl"; John Truesdell, "Truesdell in Hollywood: The Wolves Aren't So Bad," *Columbus Dispatch*, January 2, 1942; "Babs Beckwith Backs Style Pageant," *Miami News*, April 17, 1949; Blair and Blair, *Search for JFK*, 375, but they did not explain why Beckwith didn't stay in Hollywood.
206. Mason, "Glamour Girl."
207. Blair and Blair, *Search for JFK*, 371, 375.
208. Ibid., 374–76; Robertson, "Bab Was the Beauty."
209. Blair and Blair, *Search for JFK*, 371, 375; Robertson, "Bab Was the Beauty."
210. Blair and Blair, *Search for JFK*, 374–76; Maier, *Kennedys*, 166.
211. Blair and Blair, *Search for JFK*, 376.
212. "Babs Beckwith Backs Style Pageant"; "Bethany Ann Beckwith Bab" (obituary), *Miami Herald*, April 26, 2002.
213. "Bethany Ann Noble"; Martha Lummus, "Social Scenes," *Miami News*, December 6, 1948.

214. Du Manoir, "Champagne," XVI, 3–4.
215. "Bethany Ann Noble."
216. Beckwith to Sulzberger, June 16, 1952, Sulzberger to Beckwith, July 2, 1952, New York Times Company Records, Arthur Hays Sulzberger Papers, Manuscripts and Archives Division, New York Public Library; Robertson, "Bab Was the Beauty"; Blair and Blair, *Search for JFK*, 375.
217. Robertson, "Bab Was the Beauty"; genealogy for Bethany Beckwith and Alfred Corning Clark Jr., ancestry.com
218. "Cary W. Latimer Becomes a Bride at St. Patrick's," *New York Times*, May 28, 1959.
219. Du Manoir, "Champagne," XXXVII, 3; Winthrop/Frances Gardiner marriage and divorce records, ancestry.com.
220. Du Manoir, "Champagne," III, 4; XX, 3–4.
221. Ibid., III, 4; Eleanor Owens, "French Fete Adds to Weekend Gaiety," *Miami News*, February 7, 1950.
222. Martha Lummus, "Social Scenes," *Miami News*, October 5, 1949.
223. Chong, *Northern Dancer*; Martha Lummus, "Junior League Anniversary Ball," *Miami News*, December 13, 1951; Martha Lummus, "New Racing Names to Be at Hialeah," *Miami News*, September 22, 1952; Martha Lummus, "Social Register, Turf VIPs Here," *Miami News*, January 17, 1950.
224. Jobie Arnold, "Younger Set Betting on Tropical," *Miami News*, December 6, 1965; Myrna Firestone, "Trainer-Watching Has Always Been Her Best Sport," interview with Frances Luro, *Palm Beach Daily News*, March 20, 1983; "Hialeah Park Goes All Out for Flamingo Social Event," *Miami News*, February 27, 1966; "Flamingo Ball Nets $250,000," *Palm Beach Post*, March 25, 1965.
225. Minhae Shim Roth, "The Flamingo Ball, Hialeah's Historic, Celebrity-Packed Party, Returns to the Racetrack," interview with historian Paul S. George, *Miami New Times*, December 28, 2016, accessed November 22, 2017, www.miaminewtimes.com/arts/the-flamingo-ball-hialeahs-historic-celebrity-packed-party-returns-to-the-racetrack-9020052.
226. Du Manoir, "Champagne," II, 3; labeled press photo of Kelly arriving in Miami; Martha Lummus, "Brenda Frazier Kelly, Latest Celebrity to Arrive at Beach," *Miami News*, January 5, 1943.
227. Diliberto, *Debutante*, 75.
228. Ibid., 112, 141.
229. Ibid., 151; Martha Lummus, "Brenda," *Miami News*, January 5, 1943.
230. Du Manoir, "Champagne," III, 3; Lummus, "Brenda."
231. Diliberto, *Debutante*, 193, 196–98, 201–14; Cholly Knickerbocker, *Palm Beach Times*, October 30, 1952, September 13, 1952; "Italian Director Is Hustled from Brenda's Rooms," *Palm Beach Post*, November 11, 1953.
232. Diliberto, *Debutante*, 215–17, 225, 270–73.

233. Ibid., 240.
234. Paul L. Montgomery, "Brenda Frazier, Who Caught the Eye of Public as Debutante, Dies at 60," *New York Times*, May 6, 1982.
235. Du Manoir, "Champagne," V, 1, 3; VI, 1.
236. Ibid.
237. Labeled press photograph of Rosemary Warburton, author's collection.
238. "Mrs. Hugh Chisholm, Social Leader," obituary, *Philadelphia Inquirer*, August 1, 1974; "Gaynors Seeking Custody Ruling," *Palm Beach Post*, January 22, 1948; Charles Ventura, "Marital Merry-Go-Round Whirls Old Familiars from '49 Book," *Palm Beach Post*, December 3, 1948; Cholly Knickerbocker (Igor Cassini), "The Smart Set," *Palm Beach Post*, July 6, 1948.
239. "Mrs. Hugh Chisholm, Society Figure," obituary, *New York Times*, July 31, 1974.
240. Du Manoir, "Champagne," XIV, 1; XXIII, 3; "Mrs. Wiener Wins Divorce," *Miami News*, March 17, 1949.
241. "Will She Be the Third Mrs. Dempsey?," *Kansas City Times*, May 8, 1931; "Once More Jack Is Not Engaged," *Miami Herald*, January 5, 1933.
242. Du Manoir, "Champagne," XIV, 1; XXIII, 3; "Mrs. Wiener."
243. Du Manoir, "Champagne," III 4; X, 3.
244. Ibid., XV, 2; XXII, 3.
245. Reynolds and Shachtman, *Gilded Leaf*, 216, 218, 230.
246. Du Manoir, "Champagne," XV, 2; XXXIX, 3.
247. Ibid., XXII, 3.
248. Reynolds and Shachtman, *Gilded Leaf*, 244–46, 248, photographic insert.
249. Levy, *Last Playboy*, 103–10, 162, 166, 174–79.
250. Cover, *Life* magazine, January 10, 1949.
251. Pollack, *Palm Beach Visual Arts*, 90; du Manoir, "Champagne," X, 4; Milt Sosin, "Missing Patino Girl Well, Says Father Here," *Miami News*, June 15, 1954; "Nash A. Rambler," "The Tarnished Life of the 1948 Season's 'Golden Girl': Joanne Connelley Sweeny Ortiz-Patiño," Esoteric Curiosa, accessed December 16, 2017, theesotericcuriosa.blogspot.com/2010/09/tarnished-life-of-1948-season-girl_07.html.
252. "Palm Beach Foursome," *Miami News*, January 18, 1951.
253. Rambler, "Tarnished Life."
254. Levy, *Last Playboy*, 162.
255. Rambler, "Tarnished Life"; Sosin, "Missing Patino Girl."
256. Joanne Connelley Ortiz-Patino, birth and death records, ancestry.com; Rambler, "Tarnished Life"; Levy, *Last Playboy*, 311–17.
257. Du Manoir, "Champagne," XXVI, 1–2.
258. Barbara Marshall, "Brownie McLean: The Unsinkable Dowager Duchess of Palm Beach," *Palm Beach Post*, August 25, 2014; Barbara Marshall, "Brownie McLean: 100 Years of Fabulous for Palm Beach Icon," *Palm Beach Post*, July 14,

2017; reverse of Schrafft press photo; Walter Winchell, "Walter Winchell in New York," *Daytona Beach Morning Journal*, September 21, 1944; Dorothy Kilgallen, "The Voice of Broadway," *Trenton Times*, June 19, 1946.

259. Du Manoir, "Champagne," XV, 4; XXVI, 1–2; Martha Lummus, "Social Scenes," *Miami News*, October 14, 1946; Marshall, "Brownie McLean, Unsinkable"; Marshall, "100 Years."

Chapter 11

260. Du Manoir, "Champagne," XIII, 1.
261. "Joan Gentry Is Bride," *Miami News*, March 17, 1949; du Manoir, "Champagne," XI, 4.
262. Du Manoir, "Champagne," VII, 2; Walters, *Audition*, 31–32, 36–39.
263. Du Manoir, "Champagne," XXXII, 3; VI, 3; Capó, *Welcome to Fairyland*, 257; Mandy Baca, "Miami Black History: 1940s to 1960s," *New Tropic*, accessed December 20, 2017, thenewtropic.com/miami-black-history-1940s-1960s; "Deauville Club Wins Favor with Fashionable Visitors," *Miami News*, February 26, 1933.
264. Du Manoir, "Champagne," XI, 4; "Here's the Proof," political ad illustrating a letter from Miami politician citing the Brook Club, *Miami News*, April 29, 1952.
265. Du Manoir, "Champagne," XXVII, 3; Royal Palm Club, *Royal Palm Review*; "Fame and Fortune Await Winners of Great Waltz Contest," *Miami News*, November 3, 1938.
266. Royal Palm Club, *Royal Palm Review*; Austin, "When the Beach Was Hot"; Benedict, "Floridian Hotel Casino."
267. Du Manoir, "Champagne," XXVII, 3.
268. Ibid.
269. "People," *Life*, January 26, 1948, 47.
270. Du Manoir, "Champagne," XXVII, 3.
271. Ibid., XXVII, 3; XIII, 2.
272. Ibid., XIV, 2 (repeated in XIII, 3); XXVII, 3.
273. Dorothy Dey, "Night and Dey," *Miami Herald*, March 10, 1939.
274. Austin, "When the Beach Was Hot"; Royal Palm Club, *Royal Palm Review*; Helen Muir, "Madding Crowd," *Miami News*, January 8, 1938; Maude Kimball Massengale, "Mr. and Mrs. Cane Entertaining Today," *Miami Herald*, June 3, 1937; "In Miami's Realm of Social Activities," *Miami News*, December 10, 1937.
275. Du Manoir, "Champagne," IV, 3; "Giblin Refuses to Talk about Gambling Crusade," *Miami News*, February 7, 1949; United States Senate, "Special Committee on Organized Crime."
276. "Giblin Refuses to Talk"; U.S. Senate, "Special Committee on Organized Crime."

Chapter 12

277. Clipping from *El Avance Criollo*, Havana, Cuba, GLPDM Papers.
278. Du Manoir, "Champagne," XIII, 2; address book, ca. 1939; Julio C. Sanchez, residence at Sunset Island, no. 2, Miami Beach, Florida, Gottscho-Schleisner, Inc., Library of Congress Prints and Photograph Division; "Eyes of Society on Hialeah Meet," *Miami Herald*, January 8, 1939; "Others Enthused," *Miami News*, February 27, 1940.
279. Du Manoir, "La Habana, Cuba," 1–3, ca. 1940, GLPDM Papers.
280. Ibid., 3; Kemper, "Cuban Memories."
281. Somer, *Ticonderoga*, 61; "Southward Ho," *Motor Boating*, October 1939, 68; Platt, *Royal Governor*, 1.
282. Du Manoir, "Champagne," XI, 2; "Windsors Move to Biltmore, Duke Enjoys Round of Golf," *Miami News*, December 15, 1940.
283. Du Manoir, "Champagne," XVIII, 2; "Sir Harold Christie Dies at 77; Spurred Growth of Bahamas," *New York Times*, September 28, 1973.
284. Du Manoir, "Champagne," XVIII, 2.
285. Ibid., XVIII, 1.
286. Advertisement for Frank Walker, *The Scandalous Freddie McEvoy: The True Story of the Swashbuckling Australian Rogue*, Hatchette, accessed November 5, 2017, www.hachette.com.au/frank-walker/scandalous-freddie-mcevoy; Frank Walker "Heiress Divorced," *Knoxville News-Sentinel*, December 23, 1947.
287. Du Manoir, "Champagne," XVIII, 1.
288. Du Manoir, "Champagne Cocktail," November 28, 1948, 1–3.
289. Ibid.
290. du Manoir, "Champagne, Bubbles," VIII, 1.
291. Ibid., 2.
292. Ibid., 2–3.
293. Ibid., XXXI, 1.

Chapter 13

294. "Amphitheater at Beach Ready for Concert Tonight," *Miami News*, February 14, 1937; labeled press photograph of ballerina rehearsing for an outdoor dance, author's collection.
295. "Hartwick Plans Repertory for Winter Season," *Miami News*, December 15, 1935; "Drama Season to Open Jan. 6," *Charleston [WV] Gazette*, January 3, 1936.
296. "Hartwick Plans Repertory for Winter Season," *Miami News*, December 15, 1935; "Drama Season to Open Jan. 6," *Charleston [WV] Gazette*, January 3, 1936.
297. Ade to Snedigar, August 14, 1929, in Tobin, *Letters of George Ade*, 126, 142.
298. Du Manoir, "Exhibition Boada," 1941, GLPDM Papers.

299. "Art Gallery Completed at Miami Beach," *Miami News*, December 26, 1937; Pollack, *Visual Art*, 275–76.
300. Ibid.
301. Du Manoir, "Champagne," VI, 2.
302. Ibid.
303. Pollack, *Palm Beach Visual Arts*, 93; Pamela Nash Mathews, Ned Mathews's daughter, telephone interviews with author, May 1, 2014; Agnes Ash, "History," Miami newspaper clipping in the collection of Pamela Nash Mathews; du Manoir, address book; "To Promote Interest in Island Properties," *Miami News*, November 18, 1922; "Great Things Are Being Planned for the Beach in 1923," *Miami News*, December 30, 1922; "Mathews to Inspect Submerged Bay Area," *Miami Herald*, January 23, 1923.
304. Mathews interview; Ash, "History"; Pollack, *Palm Beach Visual Arts*, 93.
305. Mathews interview; Ash, "History"; Pollack, *Palm Beach Visual Arts*, 93.
306. Pollack, *Palm Beach Visual Arts*, 93.
307. Ibid. One of Benson's relatives claimed that Benson's partner in the gallery was Edward Nash Mathews Sr., not Jr., but this has since been corrected in Pollack, "Mary Duggett Benson," 21–22.
308. Ash, "History," May 1, 2014; du Manoir, "Washington Art Studio," 1941, GLPDM Papers.
309. Du Manoir, "Champagne Cocktail," November 28, 1948, 1.
310. Du Manoir, "Champagne Bubbles," XXXVII, 2; XXIX, 2; XVI, 3.
311. Du Manoir, "Champagne," XVI, 3; Mary Marley, "About People," *Miami News*, March 6, 1949.
312. Du Manoir, "Washington Art Studio"; "Franz Joseph Bolinger," obituary, *Miami Herald*, Sunday, July 27, 1986.
313. Du Manoir, "Champagne," XXIX, 3; "Spicer-Simson, Margaret (Schmidt)," in Levy, *American Art Annual*, 14: 614; University of Miami, Biographical Note.
314. Du Manoir, "Champagne," XXIX, 3; "Spicer-Simson, Margaret (Schmidt)," in Levy, *American Art Annual*, 14: 614; University of Miami, Biographical Note.
315. Du Manoir, "Champagne," XXXII, 3.
316. Ibid., XXXII, 3; "Honor Paid Author at Bookfellows Club," *Miami News*, December 7, 1949; "Sholem Asch, Author, Dies," *Miami Herald*, July 11, 1957; "Sholem Asch, 76, Author of the Nazarene, Dies," *Dallas Morning News*, July 11, 1957.
317. Du Manoir, "Champagne," XXXII, 1–3; XXVIII, 3; XVI, 3; "Lewis Vandercar," obituary, *Miami Herald*, December 17, 1988.
318. Du Manoir, "Champagne," XVI, 2; Henry L. Doherty obituary, *Miami News*, December 27, 1939.
319. Du Manoir, "Champagne," XVI, 2; "Two Janes Have Exhibit at Washington Galleries," *Miami News*, March 9, 1952.

Chapter 14

320. "Take Tables: Century Members Anticipate Frolic," *Miami Herald*, November 24, 1940.
321. Fairchild Garden, "Mission and History."
322. Du Manoir, "Champagne," XXXVIII, 1948, 1–3; Fairchild Garden, "Mission and History."
323. "Mrs. R.H. Montgomery Feted on Birthday," *Miami News*, February 24, 1948; Helen Rich, "The Guests Had a Circus at the Surf," *Miami News*, February 25, 1957.
324. Trumbull, *Twins' Sister*, 120, loc. 1477; "Molly O'Daniel Danielson," obituary, *Los Angeles Times*, August 28, 1996, accessed November 28 2017, articles.latimes.com/1996-08-28/local/me-38343_1_santa-barbara.
325. Trumbull, *Twins' Sister*, 120, loc. 1477.
326. De Lewenhaupt to Herb Rau, reprinted in Rau, "Miami Mishmash," *Miami News*, February 17, 1964; Don Branning, "Night Beat," *Miami News*, July 14, 1963; "Oil Portraits and Other Fine Items from the Estate of a Count and Countess from Sweden Will Be Sold Aug. 10 in Florida," ArtfixDaily.com, July 29, 2013, accessed November 12, 2017, www.artfixdaily.com/artwire/release/1869-oil-portraits-and-other-fine-items-from-the-estate-of-a-count-and.

Chapter 15

327. Du Manoir, "Within the Social Circle," November 4, 1948, 1.
328. Du Manoir, "Champagne," December 1948, XXXIX, 2.
329. Ibid., I, 2–3; Fisher to Muir, May 14, 1953, Helen Muir Papers, University of Miami Library.
330. Du Manoir, "Champagne," XXXIX, 2; Cholly Knickerbocker, *Palm Beach Post-Times*, October 17, 1952.
331. Du Manoir, "Within," 3; "Champagne," XXXIX, 2; XXXV, ca. December 25, 1948, 3; Martha Lummus, "Social Scenes," *Miami News*, December 6, 1948.
332. Du Manoir, "Within," 2; "Champagne," XXVII, 3; XIII, 2.
333. Sam Roberts, "Aileen Mehle, Gossip's Grande Dame Known as 'Suzy,' Dies at 98," *New York Times*, November 11, 2016.
334. Du Manoir, "Within," 2; "Champagne," XXXIX, 2.
335. Du Manoir, "Champagne," XXXIV, 3.
336. *Broadway Brevities*, "Miss Joan Sawyer," 36; Russ Shor, "Joan Sawyer, Jazz Vampire," accessed December 3, 2017, www.vjm.biz/161-joan-sawyer.pdf.
337. "Slight Difference," *Seattle Daily Times*, October 17, 1916.
338. *Broadway Brevities*, "Miss Joan Sawyer," 36; Shor, "Sawyer, Jazz."
339. Shor, "Sawyer, Jazz"; Winona Wilcox, "Art Versus Love Seen in Triangle," *Cincinnati Post*, December 23, 1916; "The Other Woman Speaks," *Kansas City Star*,

August 20, 1917; "Chilean Beauty Almost Faints at 'Not Guilty,'" *New Orleans Item*, December 2, 1917.
340. Sawyer to *New York World*, reprinted in "Other Woman."
341. *Broadway Brevities*, "Miss Joan Sawyer," 35, 36, 40.
342. *Broadway Brevities*, "Miss Joan Sawyer"; Shor, "Sawyer, Jazz"; "Woman Sued for Wife's Estrangement," *Palm Beach Post*, December 15, 1929; B. Joan Rentschler, Florida marriage and divorce records, ancestry.com.
343. "Miami Beach Brevities," *Miami News*, January 25, 1928; "Midwinter Scene at Fleetwood Hotel Colorful Panorama," *Miami News*, February 24, 1935; "Missing Gems Trouble Police," *Miami News*, November 24, 1941; "There It Was!" *Palm Beach Post*, November 25, 1921.
344. "J.G. Kiley, Miamian, Married Today," *Miami News*, February 29, 1944; Kleinberg, *Miami Beach*, 34; Fisher, *Pacesetter*, loc. 1137; Redford, *Billion-Dollar Sandbar*, 61.
345. "Wife Accuses Story Writer," *Miami News*, June 17, 1944.
346. Du Manoir, "Champagne," XXXIII, 1–3.
347. Ibid., XXIX, 3.
348. Ibid., XIII, 3–4.

Chapter 16

349. Du Manoir, Champagne, IV, un-paginated insert.
350. Du Manoir, insert; Mary Wallace, "The Art of Taking It Off," *Miami News*, March 27, 1949.
351. Du Manoir, insert.
352. Gwen Harrison, "Conversation Piece," *Miami Herald*, October 20, 1950.
353. Du Manoir, "Champagne," II, 5–6; Harrison, "Conversation Piece."
354. Du Manoir, "Champagne," I, 2–3.
355. Ibid., XXXIV, 2–3.
356. Ibid., IV, 1.
357. Ibid., III, 5.

Chapter 17

358. "Set New Records," *Miami Herald*, April 28, 1940.
359. Clipping, GLPDM Papers; "Rich Woman to Prosecute Valerie Scott," *Seattle Times*, March 9, 1942.
360. Labeled press photograph, March 1949, author's collection.
361. C.G. Berning, "Mrs. Bellous Says She Was More than Secretary to Gar Wood," *Miami Herald*, October 28, 1949; Don Petit, "Mrs. Bellous in Illinois, Secretary's Attorney Says," *Miami News*, October 25, 1949; "Mrs. Bellous in Miami; Denies

Hiding," *Miami News*, November 6, 1949; William C. Baggs, "Wood More than Boss, Sued Secretary Relates," *Miami News*, October 28, 1949. All of these reports, including quotes, came from Bellous's legal answer.
362. C.G. Berning, "Mrs. Bellous Says She Was More than Secretary to Gar Wood," *Miami Herald*, October 28, 1949; Don Petit, "Mrs. Bellous in Illinois, Secretary's Attorney Says," *Miami News*, October 25, 1949; "Mrs. Bellous in Miami; Denies Hiding," *Miami News*, November 6, 1949; William C. Baggs, "Wood More than Boss, Sued Secretary Relates," *Miami News*, October 28, 1949. All of these reports, including quotes, came from Bellous's legal answer.
363. C.G. Berning, "Mrs. Bellous Says She Was More than Secretary to Gar Wood," *Miami Herald*, October 28, 1949; Don Petit, "Mrs. Bellous in Illinois, Secretary's Attorney Says," *Miami News*, October 25, 1949; "Mrs. Bellous in Miami; Denies Hiding," *Miami News*, November 6, 1949; William C. Baggs, "Wood More than Boss, Sued Secretary Relates," *Miami News*, October 28, 1949. All of these reports, including quotes, came from Bellous's legal answer.
364. "G.A. Wood & Co., Wood Hydraulic Hoist (& Body Co.), Gar Wood Industries," Coachbuilt, accessed March 18, 2018, www.coachbuilt.com/bui/g/gar_wood/gar_wood.htm.
365. Berning, "Mrs. Bellous Says"; Petit, "Mrs. Bellous in Illinois"; Baggs, "Wood More than Boss." Quote is again from the attorney's legal answer to Wood's lawsuit.
366. William C. Baggs, "Receiver Hunts Gar Wood's Cash," *Miami News*, October 19, 1949.
367. Ibid.; C.G. Berning, "Custodian Named in Wood Suit," *Miami Herald*, October 21, 1949.
368. Baggs, "Receiver Hunts Gar Wood's Cash"; Berning, "Mrs. Bellous Says"; labeled press photograph of Bellous giving legal answer to Bandel, November 8, 1949, author's collection.
369. "Gar Wood's Suit against Woman Ended," *Miami News*, January 27, 1950; Florida Bar, *Florida Bar Journal* 42 (1968): 1092.
370. Milt Sosin, "Millionaire Dead at Ninety, Brother Recalls the Early Years," *Miami News*, June 21, 1971.
371. Ibid.; "Model Says Gar Set Her Adrift," *Miami News*, December 1, 1954; "Gar Wood in Court," *Beaumont* (TX) *Journal*, December 16, 1954.
372. Austin, "When the Beach Was Hot"; Joan Nielsen, "Miami Memo," *Miami News*, June 1, 1954; Joan Nielsen, "Another Astor Party," *Miami News*, January 27, 1956.
373. Sanford Schnier, "Police Seize Model for Plaguing Astor," *Miami News*, December 26, 1956; "Police Hunt Astor on Pretty Model's Charge," *Miami News*, December 29, 1956.
374. "She Had a Tough Night," *Miami News*, February 12, 1957.

375. "J.J. Astor's 'Shadow' Gets Out of Jail," *Miami News*, February 14, 1957; labeled press photograph, February 12, 1957, author's collection.
376. "Astor Romance Leads to Suit," *Stars and Stripes*, July 26, 1957; "Astor Loses Plea to Bar Woman's Suit," *Herald-Statesman* (Yonkers), July 26, 1957.
377. John Fix, "Gar Wood: An Old Sea Dog Is Up to New Tricks," *Popular Mechanics*, July 1967, 82–84; "Gar Jr. Fights for a Fortune," interview with Wood's son, *Miami News*, August 9, 1973.
378. Alice, "Through the Looking Glass," *Miami News*, March 21, 1952.
379. Thomas Sopwith, quoted in Joslyn and Malinovska, *Voices of Flight*, 225–27; du Manoir, address book; Helen Rich, "Notebook," *Miami News*, December 20, 1937; "Palm Beach Notes," *Palm Beach Post*, December 22, 1937; "Windsors Move Home during Alterations," *Palm Beach Post*, August 25, 1940.
380. Charles van Deusen, "Runaway Lovers," *Boston American*, March 31, 1957.
381. Labeled press photograph, February 5, 1957, author's collection; "Heiress Sets 3rd Wedding," *Omaha World-Herald*, February 1, 1957.
382. "Sigrist Heir Expects Stork in December," *Miami News*, April 25, 1957; "Regains Child's Custody," *Marietta (GA) Journal*, July 27, 1958.
383. "Lady Beatrice Ormerod," Find-a-Grave, accessed April 4, 2018, www.findagrave.com/memorial/143693057/beatrice-ormerod.

Chapter 18

384. Pollack, *Palm Beach Visual Arts*, 73–84, 86–90, 123–25.
385. Fisher, deposition, 5–6.
386. Ibid., 3–5.
387. Ibid.
388. Ibid.; Klein, decision.
389. Fisher, deposition, 7.
390. Ibid., 2.
391. Ibid. By then, Fisher had moved to 5120 Lakeview Drive.
392. Klein, decision.
393. "Sandwiches by the Thousands," *Miami News*, December 7, 1957.
394. Herb Rau, "The Shooting Is Over," *Miami News*, November 19, 1958.
395. Robert Gifford, death records, ancestry.com; Margaret Acer, "You Can Spot US Woman Anywhere," *Miami News*, June 14, 1959.
396. Margaret Acer, "Party Line," *Miami News*, August 4, 1960; Margaret Acer, "What's Slim, Trim, and Lost?" *Miami News*, June 3, 1960.
397. Bremser, *Advertising Miami*, 45; Joan Nielsen McHale, "Scene and Heard," *Miami News*, March 14, 1962.
398. Kearsley and Westervelt, interviews with author, October 11, 2017, January 30, 2018; "Dolly Says," *Miami News*, December 2, 1937.

399. Leone King, "Palm Beach Notes," *Palm Beach Post*, August 8, 1964; Rieta Brabham Langhorne Westervelt/du Manoir marriage records, ancestry.com.
400. Westervelt, telephone interview with author, October 11, 2017.
401. Kearsley interviews with author, October 11, 2017, January 30, 2017.
402. Redford, *Billion-Dollar Sandbar*, 274–75; Magic City History, "Jane Fisher Passes Away."
403. Rieta Westervelt, du Manoir death records, ancestry.com.

BIBLIOGRAPHY

Aeronautical Industry. "Airports." November 1930.

Armbruster, Ann. *The Life and Times of Miami Beach.* New York: Knopf, 1995.

Austin, Tom. *The Surf Club.* New York: Assouline, 2013.

———. "When the Beach Was Hot." *Miami New Times*, February 3, 1993. Accessed January 14, 2018. www.miaminewtimes.com/news/when-the-beach-was-hot-6362394.

Baca, Mandy. "Miami Black History: 1940s to 1960s." *The New Tropic.* Accessed December 20, 2017. thenewtropic.com/miami-black-history-1940s-1960s.

Baker, Charles H., Jr. *Jigger, Beaker and Glass: Drinking Around the World.* Lanham, MD: Derrydale Press, 1992.

Ballinger, Kenneth. *Miami Millions: The Dance of the Dollars in the Great Florida Land Boom of 1925.* Miami: Franklin Press, 1936.

Banta, R.E. *Indiana Authors and Their Books: 1816–1916.* Crawfordsville, IN: Wabash College, 1949.

Beck, Simon D. *The Aircraft-Spotter's Film and Television Companion.* Jefferson, NC: McFarland, 2016.

Benedict, John. "Floridian Casino, Miami Beach, Florida, 1929–1930." Museum of Gaming History. Accessed February 2, 2018. museumofgaminghistory.org/mogh_article.php?a=29.

Bergen Community College. "About Emil Buehler." Accessed December 21, 2018. bergen.edu/academics/academic-divisions-departments/computer-scienceinformationengineeringtechnologies/aviation-program/about-emil-buehler.

Biondi, Joan. *Miami Beach Memories: A Nostalgic Chronicle of Days Gone By.* Guilford, CT: Globe Pequot Press, 2006.

Blair, Joan, and Clay Blair. *The Search for JFK.* New York: Berkley, 1976.

Bibliography

Bramson, Seth. *Burdines: Sunshine Fashions and the Florida Store.* Charleston, SC: The History Press, 2011.

———. *Miami Beach.* Charleston, SC: Arcadia Publishing, 2005.

———. *Sunshine, Stone Crabs and Cheesecake: The Story of Miami Beach.* Charleston, SC: The History Press, 2009.

Bremser, George, Jr., ed. *Advertising Miami.* Miami: Advertising Club of Greater Miami, 1961.

British Movietone. "Mr. Churchill in Miami." YouTube. Accessed January 6, 2018. www.youtube.com/watch?v=-318chn-IiU.

Broadway Brevities. "Miss Joan Sawyer." April 1921.

Capó, Julio, Jr. *Welcome to Fairyland: Queer Miami before 1940.* Chapel Hill: University of North Carolina Press, 2017.

Carrozza, Anthony R. *William D. Pawley: The Extraordinary Life of the Adventurer, Entrepreneur, and Diplomat Who Founded the Flying Tigers.* Washington, D.C.: Potomac Books, 2012.

Carson, Ruby Leach. "Forty Years of Miami Beach." *Tequesta* no. 15 (1955): 3–27.

Chong, Kevin. *Northern Dancer: The Legendary Horse That Inspired a Nation.* New York: Viking, 2014.

Christies, New York. *Fine Printed Books and Manuscripts.* Sale 24456, June 23, 2011.

City of Miami Beach Planning Department. *Collins Waterfront Historic District Designation Report.* Miami Beach: City of Miami Beach, 2000. PDF, accessed March 3, 2018. www.miamibeachfl.gov/wp-content/uploads/2017/08/Collins-Waterfront.pdf.

Davis, Ronald L. *Hollywood Beauty: Linda Darnell and the American Dream.* Norman: University of Oklahoma Press, 1991.

Diliberto, Gioia. *Debutante: The Story Behind Brenda Frazier.* New York: Pocket Books, 1988.

Doner, Michele Oka. *Miami Beach: Blueprint of an Eden.* New York: Harper Design, 2007.

Doyle, William Stoner. "Carl Fisher: Builder of Miami." *Coronet Magazine*, 1949.

du Manoir, George Le Pelley. Address book, ca. 1939. GLPDM Papers.

———. "Blimping Along Over Miami Beach." Typewritten article, 1940. GLPDM Papers.

———. "Champagne Bubbles." Forty typewritten essays, 1948–49. GLPDM Papers.

———. "Champagne Cocktail." Typewritten article, November 28, 1948. GLPDM Papers.

———. "Exhibition Boada." Typewritten article, 1941. GLPDM Papers.

———. "Hialeah Luncheon." Typewritten article, ca. 1941. GLPDM Papers.

———. "Humane Society." Typewritten article, ca. 1941. GLPDM Papers.

———. "La Habana, Cuba." Typewritten article, 1940. GLPDM Papers.

Bibliography

———. "Miami Beach." Various essays, 1935. GLPDM Papers.

———. "The 'Versailles.'" Typewritten article, 1941. GLPDM Papers.

———. "Washington Art Studio." Typewritten article, ca. 1940. GLPDM Papers.

———. "What about Going Hunting?" Typewritten article, ca. 1940. GLPDM Papers.

———. "Within the Social Circle." Typewritten article, November 21, 1948. GLPDM Papers.

Fairchild Garden. "Fairchild Garden: Mission and History." Accessed November 11, 2017. www.fairchildgarden.org/About-Fairchild/Mission-History.

Farrell, Eileen, and Brian Kellow. *Can't Help Singing: The Life of Eileen Farrell.* Lebanon, NH: Northeastern University Press, 1999.

Fisher, Jane. Deposition on behalf of George du Manoir, in re: Trust Under Deed of Evelyn Chew Gifford, May 15, 1958. GLPDM Papers.

———. *Fabulous Hoosier: A Story of American Achievement.* New York: McBride, 1947.

———. Last Will and Testament of Jane Fisher, July 21, 1967. Miami-Dade County Clerk's Office.

Fisher, Jerry. *The Pacesetter: The Complete Story.* Victoria, BC Canada: FriesenPress, 2014. Kindle.

Fix, John. "Gar Wood: An Old Sea Dog Is Up to New Tricks." *Popular Mechanics*, July 1967.

Florida Death Index, 1877–1998. Ancestry.com.

Florida Divorce Index, 1927–2001. Ancestry.com.

Florida Marriage Index, 1927–2001. Ancestry.com.

Four Seasons Press Room. "The Four Seasons Hotel at the Surf Club in Surfside, Florida, Is Now Open." Four Seasons Hotel, PDF press release, March 23, 2017.

Garcia, Rafael R. "The First International Sky Train Flight." *Airpost Journal*, June 1935.

George, Paul S. *Along the Miami River.* Charleston, SC: Arcadia Publishing, 2013.

———. "Brokers, Binders and Builders: Greater Miami's Boom of the Mid-1920s." *Florida Historical Quarterly* 55, no. 2 (July 1986): 27–51.

Gilbert, Martin. *Churchill: A Life.* New York: Holt, 1992.

Gittelman. Steven H. *Willie K. Vanderbilt II: A Biography.* Jefferson, NC: McFarland, 2010.

HistoryMiami. "The Committee of 100." Accessed October 19, 2017. www.historymiami.org/fastspot/get-involved/committee-of-100/index.html.

Holston, Kim R. *Richard Widmark: A Bio-bibliography.* Westport, CT: Greenwood Publishing Group, 1990.

Indiana Marriage Index, 1800–1941. Ancestry.com.

Joslyn, Mauriel, and Anna Malinovska. *Voices of Flight: Conversations with Air Veterans of the Great War.* Barnsley, UK: Pen and Sword, 2006.

Kaiser, Charles. *The Gay Metropolis: The Landmark History of Gay Life in America.* New York: Grove Press, 2007.

BIBLIOGRAPHY

Kelley, Etna M. "Steve Hannagan Gives First Place to the Camera in Publicity." *Popular Photography*, June 1944.

Kemper, Rudo. "Cuban Memories: The Cuban Constitution of 1940, Then and Today." Cuban Heritage Collection, University of Miami, October 14, 2010. Accessed October 26, 2017. library.miami.edu/chc/2010/10/14/cuban-memories-the-cuban-constitution-of-1940-then-and-today.

Klein, Judge J.P. Decision, Gifford Estate, No. 2146 of 1957, 18 Pa. D. & C. 2d 769 (1959), November 6, 1959, Common Pleas Court of Philadelphia County, Pennsylvania, Leagle. Accessed November 12, 2017. www.leagle.com/decision/195978718padampc2d7691644.

Kleinberg, Howard. *Miami Beach: A History.* Miami: Centennial Press, 1994.

———. *Miami: The Way We Were.* Surfside, FL: Surfside Publications, 1989.

Kleinberg, Howard, and Carolyn Klepser. *Miami Beach: A Centennial History.* Edited by Arva Moore Parks. Miami: Global, 2016.

Klepser, Carolyn. *Lost Miami Beach.* Charleston, SC: The History Press, 2014.

Lavender, Abraham D. *Miami Beach in 1920: The Making of a Winter Resort.* Charleston, SC: Arcadia Publishing, 2002.

Leigh, Virginia, with William J. Slocum. "The Debutante Industry." *Collier's Weekly*, October 23, 1948.

Lenburg, Jeff. *Peekaboo: The Story of Veronica Lake.* New York: St. Martin's Press, 1983. Reprint Lincoln, NE: iUniverse, 2001.

Levy, Florence Nightingale, ed. *American Art Annual* 14 (1917). Washington, D.C.: American Federation of Arts.

Levy, Shawn. *The Last Playboy: The High Life of Porfirio Rubirosa.* New York: HarperCollins, 2005.

Life. "Fishermen Get Away from It All at a Club Knee-Deep in Biscayne Bay." February 10, 1941.

———. "The Impeccable Blandford." January 17, 1949.

———. "Natural History: Hialeah Race Track Flamingos at Last Hatch Flock of Chicks." June 19, 1939.

———. "People." January 26, 1948.

Lowe Art Museum, University of Miami. "History." Accessed November 16, 2017. www6.miami.edu/lowe/history.html.

Magic City History. "Jane Fisher Passes Away in 1968." Accessed December 23, 2017. miami-history.com/news/jane-fisher-passes-away-in-1950.

Maier, Thomas. *The Kennedys: America's Emerald Kings: A Five-Generation History of the Ultimate Irish-Catholic Family.* New York: Basic Books, 2009.

Malvy, Louis, to du Manoir, February 1937. GLPDM Papers.

McIver, Stuart B. *Dreamers Schemers and Scalawags: The Florida Chronicles.* Vol. 1. Sarasota, FL: Pineapple Press, 1998.

Bibliography

"The Merrill-Magowan Family." Five College Archives and Manuscript Collections, Series 1. Amherst College Archives and Special Collections, Amherst, Massachusetts. Accessed November 15, 2017. asteria.fivecolleges.edu/findaids/amherst/ma207_list.html.

Mockler, Kim I. *Maurice Fatio: Palm Beach Architect.* New York: Acanthus Press, 2010.

Motor Boating. "Thomas J. Pancoast." November 1941.

Murrell, Muriel V. *Miami: A Backward Glance.* Sarasota, FL: Pineapple Press, 2003.

New York Times Company Records. Arthur Hays Sulzberger Papers, Manuscripts and Archives Division, New York Public Library.

Nijman, Jan. *Miami: Mistress of the Americas.* Philadelphia: University of Pennsylvania Press, 2010.

Parks, Arva Moore. *Miami: The Magic City.* Miami: Community Media, 2008.

Parks, Arva Moore, and Carolyn Klepser. *Miami Then and Now.* London: Pavilion, 2014.

Platt, Owen. *The Royal Governor and the Duchess: The Duke and Duchess of Windsor in the Bahamas 1940–1945.* Lincoln, NE: iUniverse, 2003.

Pollack, Deborah C. "Mary Duggett Benson and Her Iconic Worth Avenue Gallery." *Tustenegee,* Historical Society of Palm Beach County journal 9, no. 1 (Spring 2018): 19–25.

———. *Palm Beach Visual Arts.* Gretna, LA: Pelican Publishing, 2016.

———. *Visual Art and the Urban Evolution of the New South.* Columbia: University of South Carolina Press, 2015.

"Rambler, Nash A." "The Tarnished Life of the 1948 Season's 'Golden Girl': Joanne Connelley Sweeny Ortiz-Patiño." The Esoteric Curiosa. Accessed December 16, 2017. theesotericcuriosa.blogspot.com/2010/09/tarnished-life-of-1948-season-girl_07.html.

Redford, Polly. *Billion-Dollar Sandbar: A Biography of Miami Beach.* New York: Dutton, 1970.

———. Interview with Alfred Barton, May 18, 1967. University of Florida Oral History Project, University of Florida digital collections. Accessed October 23, 2017. ufdc.ufl.edu/UF00006423/00001.

———. Interview with Charles W. "Pete" Chase, October 1971. University of Florida digital collections. Accessed April 2, 2018. ufdc.ufl.edu/UF00025921/00001.

———. Interview with Jane Fisher, April 4, 1967. University of Florida Oral History Project, University of Florida digital collections. Accessed October 23, 2017. ufdc.ufl.edu/UF00025926/00001.

———. Interview with Russell Pancoast, May 15, 1967. University of Florida Oral History Project, University of Florida digital collections. Accessed November 5, 2017. ufdc.ufl.edu/UF00006422/00001.

Reynolds, Patrick, and Tom Shachtman. *The Gilded Leaf: Triumph, Tragedy, and Tobacco: Three Generations of the R.J. Reynolds Family and Fortune.* Boston: Little Brown, 1989. Reprint, Backinprint.com, 2006.

Bibliography

Rolfes, Hans. *General Foods: America's Premier Food Company*. Poughkeepsie, NY: Hudson House, 2007.

Roth, Minhae Shim. "The Flamingo Ball, Hialeah's Historic, Celebrity-Packed Party, Returns to the Racetrack." Interview with Paul George, historian, *Miami New Times*, December 28, 2016. Accessed November 22, 2017. www.miaminewtimes.com/arts/the-flamingo-ball-hialeahs-historic-celebrity-packed-party-returns-to-the-racetrack-9020052.

Royal Palm Club. *The Royal Palm Review of 1940*. Miami: Royal Palm Club.

Sertel, Lino L., ed. *Social Register of Miami*. Miami: Blue Book, 1940.

Soames, Mary. *Clementine Churchill: The Biography of a Marriage*. New York: Houghton Mifflin/Harcourt, 2003.

Social Security Death Index. Ancestry.com.

Somer, Jack A. *Ticonderoga: Tales of an Enchanted Yacht*. Mystic, CT: Mystic Seaport, 1997.

Time. "Florida: Pleasure Dome." February 19, 1940.

Tobin, Terrence, ed. *Letters of George Ade*. West Lafayette, IN: Purdue University Press, 1998.

Trenham, Peter C. "A Chronicle of the Philadelphia Section PGA and Golf in the Philadelphia Area." Trenham Golf History. Accessed November 9, 2017. trenhamgolfhistory.org/Leaders19221929.html.

Trumbull, Louise. *The Twins' Sister*. Bloomington, IN: XLibris, 2011. Kindle.

United States Senate. "Special Committee on Organized Crime in Interstate Commerce." Washington, D.C.: United States Senate. Accessed January 14, 2018. www.senate.gov/artandhistory/history/common/investigations/Kefauver.htm.

Universal Newspaper News Reel. "Dusky Entertainers a Feature of Annual Millionaires' Outing." Ca. 1931, Critical Past, YouTube. Accessed November 1, 2017. www.youtube.com/watch?v=5bAtHHzehVk.

University of Miami. Theodore Spicer-Simson Collection: Biographical Note. Accessed December 1, 2017. proust.library.miami.edu/findingaids/?p=collections/findingaid&id=135.

Walters, Barbara. *Audition: A Memoir*. New York: Knopf, 2008.

White, Philip. *Churchill's Cold War*. London: Bloomsbury, Duckworth Overlook, 2012.

Wright, E. Lynne. *More than Petticoats: Remarkable Florida Women*. Guilford, CT: Globe Pequot, 2001. Reprint 2010.

INDEX

A

Ade, George 119
African Americans 16, 24, 109, 132
All American Fashion Pageant
    Committee 94
Alton Road 19, 73
Alva Base 85
Arden, Elizabeth 36
Art Deco 55, 57, 59, 120, 152
Asch, Sholem 125
Astor, John Jacob, VI 131, 145
aviation 14, 15, 23, 47, 49, 83, 86, 92,
    147, 153

B

backgammon 36
Bandel, Louie (Louis) 143
Barnett, Marta 42
Barnett, Robert T. "Bob" 33
Barron, Herman 35
Barton, Alfred Ilko 23, 24, 30, 88, 119,
    127, 131, 136, 139
Barton, Sallie Cobb "Cobbie" 28,
    30, 139

Baruch, Bernard, Jr. 42
Baruch, Bernard, Sr. 42
Baruch, Sailing 42
Bass Museum of Art 120
Bath and Tennis Club 24, 38, 40, 42
Bath Club 21, 24, 34, 74, 80, 93, 122
Beachcomber 80
Beckwith, Bethany Ann "Babs" 90, 92,
    93, 94, 110, 111
Beckwith, Dr. Jesse Holden 90, 92
Belle Isle 122
Bellous, Violet 141, 143, 146
Benson, Mary Duggett 123
Biltmore Country Club 23, 36, 42,
    115, 127
Biscayne Bay 33, 36, 38, 39, 68, 73, 83,
    107, 127, 130
Biscayne Palace, Miami 76
Boada Martin, Fernando 120
Boeing Company 153
Bohland, Gustav 120
Boles, John 57
Bolinger, Franz Josef "Joe" 124
Brian, Mary 55
bridge (card game) 36, 38
Bromley, Dorothy 65

INDEX

Brook Club 111
Brown, Avritt 124
Buehler, Emil 83
Burdine's 36

C

canasta 38
Capone, Al 108, 110
card games 36, 38
Cardozo Hotel 152
Carillon Hotel 129, 150
Carlberg, Eric 123, 124
Carroll, Nancy 124
Casa Alva 64
Cassini, Igor 42, 139
Castle, Irene 109, 131
Chase, Ilka 88
Chevallier, Jacques 136
Childers, Arthur 110, 112
Chisholm, Rosemary Warburton Gaynor 99, 101
Christie, Sir Harold 97, 115
Christy, Howard Chandler 21
Chrysler, Walter P., Jr. 30
Churchill, Clementine 59, 64
Churchill, Sarah 61
Churchill, Sir Winston 59, 60, 61, 64, 110, 115, 124
Clark, Attorney General Tom C. 131
Clarke, Colonel Frank 59, 60, 61, 64, 110
Clark, John C. 30, 61, 65
Clark, Kay 96
Clover Club 109
Club Boheme 54, 102, 109
Cluett, William G. 40
Coconut Grove 125
Coconut Grove Playhouse 82
Collins Avenue 68, 102, 119, 120, 150
Collins, John 26, 34
Colonial Inn 138
Colony Hotel, Palm Beach 104
Colony restaurant, New York City 97, 139

Committee of 100 16, 24, 34, 119
Connelley, Joanne 104, 106, 110
Cooper, Clayton Sedgwick 16, 23, 119
Cooper, Gary 88
Copps, Joe 68
Coral Gables 26, 36, 94, 115, 124, 127, 128
Count Fleet 68
Cowell, Ione Staley 53
Cowell, Shirley 53, 54, 94, 138
Cox, Governor James Middleton 35
Crandon, Charles H. 128
Crane, Doris 36
Crozer, Marion. *See* Sailer, Marion Crozer
Cuban painting 124
Cuban photography 120
Cuban sculpture 120
Cuban Tourist Commission 120

D

Danielson, Dick 129
Danielson, Molly 129
Darnell, Linda 74, 76
Deauville Club 108
Deauville Hotel 108
debutantes 33, 88, 97, 99, 104, 110, 136
Deering, James 127
de la Fregonniere, Countess (Priscilla Dickerson) 98
de la Fregonniere, Count Guy 98, 116
de Lewenhaupt, Count Claes Eric 129
de Lewenhaupt, Countess Eugenia 129
de Moya, Angel 120
Dempsey, Jack 101
de Saulles, Blanca 132, 133, 134
de Saulles, John 132
de Toth, Andre 74, 76
de Trafford, Sir Humphrey 65
Dickerson, Edward Nicoll 24, 98
Dietrich, Marlene 54
Di Lido Island 42
Dodd, Ruth 101

INDEX

Doherty, Henry L. 127
Dorelis, Count José 68
Dorelis, Dolly Hemingway
    Fleischmann O'Brien 70
Douglas, Marjory Stoneman 128, 129
Duke, Anthony Drexel 116
du Manoir, Count George Le Pelley
    13, 14, 15, 16, 19, 20, 21, 23, 24,
    28, 30, 33, 36, 38, 39, 42, 45, 47,
    52, 53, 55, 58, 59, 64, 65, 68, 73,
    74, 79, 83, 88, 94, 96, 97, 99,
    101, 104, 106, 108, 110, 111,
    117, 118, 119, 120, 124, 125,
    127, 128, 129, 130, 131, 136,
    138, 141, 145, 146, 150, 152,
    153, 154
du Manoir, Yves Le Pelley 13
DuPont company 47
du Pont, Éleuthère Paul, Jr. 47, 49, 50
du Pont, Helena Allaire Crozer 47, 52
du Pont, Richard Chichester 47, 52

E

Eden Roc 150
Eisenhower, Dwight David 53, 96
Embassy Club, Miami 139
Evans, Roy 138
Everglades 46, 124
Everglades Club 38, 40, 104

F

Faena, Alan 57
Fairchild, David 124, 128
Fairchild, Marian 125, 128
Fairchild Tropical Botanic Garden
    128, 129
Fanjul family 113
Farrell, Glenda 82
fashion shows 36, 94, 138
Fatio, Maurice 31, 74
Figueroa, Jorge B. 120
Filatre, Claude Stephanie 116
Fink, Denman 26

Firestone, Elizabeth (Betty) Parke 52
Firestone, Harvey Samuel, Jr. 52
Firestone, Harvey Samuel, Sr. 16, 24, 52
Firestone, Roger Stanley 52
Firestone (Willis), Elizabeth 53
Fisher, Carl Graham 16, 20, 24, 35, 68,
    74, 85, 134
Fisher Island 85, 99, 141
Fisher Island Club 85
Fisher, Jane 20, 29, 96, 127, 130, 139,
    150, 152, 154
fishing 36, 39, 113
Flamingo Ball 96, 131
Flamingo Hotel 16, 55, 83
Flamingo Park 119
Flamingo Stakes 71, 96
Fleetwood Hotel 83, 134
Florida Keys 117
Flynn, Errol 39, 110, 116
Fontainebleau 52, 54, 150, 152
Four Seasons Hotel at the Surf Club 31
Frazier (Kelly), Brenda 97, 98, 99

G

Gable, Clark 58, 70
gambling 36, 109, 110, 111, 112,
    115, 116
Gambridge Club 38
Gardiner, Frances Weinman Latimer.
    See Luro, Frances
Gardiner, Winthrop "Winnie" 92, 94,
    108, 110
Gardner, Francis Howell 141
Gaynor, William Charles Thomas 99
Gentry, Joan. *See* O'Neill, Joan Gentry
    Shelden
Gershwin, George 109
Gifford, Evelyn Chew 15, 19, 24, 34,
    58, 73, 111, 119, 140, 150, 152
Gifford, Robert W. 15, 16, 19, 23,
    24, 34, 57, 73, 111, 119, 140,
    150, 152
Giller, Norman 150

Index

Gilman, James 140
gin rummy 38
Goldwyn, Samuel 94
golf 31, 35, 36
Gondolier 23, 45, 83
Gonzales, Ricardo Alonso (Richard) "Pancho" 43
Goodyear blimp 83, 84, 85
Greene, Bob 129
Greene, Nancy 129
Gubelmann, Walter 116
Guest, C.Z. 101, 104

H

Hagen, Walter 35
Haitian paintings 124
Hallandale 138
Hall, Jon 80
Hannagan, Steve 68, 139
Hasbrouck, Lucille Mellon 24
Havana, Cuba 49, 61, 113, 152
Haviland, Lieutenant Colonel William D. 86
Hawker Aircraft Company 147
Hearst, Randolph A. Hearst 93
Henie, Sonja 95, 108
Hertz, Frances "Fannie" 68
Hertz, John D., Jr. 110
Hertz, John D., Sr. 68
Hialeah Park pink flamingos 71, 72
Hialeah Park Race Track 30, 45, 52, 61, 64, 65, 68, 71, 96, 98, 104
Hibiscus Island 125
Hispanic culture 113, 120, 153
HistoryMiami Museum 21, 97
Hobe Sound 153
Hole in the Head, A 152
Holiday, Billie 109
Hollywood, California 54, 74, 76, 79, 82, 94
Honeywell, Mark C. 34, 117
Hoover, J. Edgar 131
Hopper, Hedda 76
Horne, Lena 53
horse racing 52, 65, 68, 71, 96
Horton, Edward Everett 81, 82
Hubbell, Henry Salem 16
Hufty, Page 40
Hughes, Howard 53, 94
hunting 45, 46
hurricanes 73
Husing, Ted 139

I

Igleheart, Phyllis. *See* Kerdasha, Phyllis Igleheart
Indian Creek Country Club 28, 31, 33, 107
Indian Creek Island 31, 141

J

Jewish Floridian 82
Jews 24, 35, 126
Jones, Bobby 33
Juarez, Gregg 147, 149
Jupiter Island 153

K

Kearsley, Martha L. 153
Kefauver, Estes 112
Kellogg, John Harvey 16
Kelso 52
Kennedy, Jacqueline 93, 96
Kennedy, John Fitzgerald 93
Kerdasha, Phyllis Igleheart 28
Key Largo 117
Key Largo Anglers Club 118, 127
Key West 117
Kiley, John Gerald "Jed" 134, 136
Kilkenny, Captain Thomas "Ted" 128
King Cole Hotel 55, 71, 88
Kunkel, Raymond 40

Index

L

La Gorce Country Club 35, 81
La Gorce Island 131
La Gorce, John Oliver 34, 35
Lake, Veronica 74, 76
Langford, Frances 79, 80
Lansky, Meyer 112
Lapidus, Morris 150
Leigh, Virginia 110
Levi, Mayor John Hale 134
Lincoln Road 64, 94, 101, 115, 124, 136
Lindenberg, Enid Lee 88, 90
Little Palm Club 110
London, England 134, 147
Love, J. Spencer 40
Luro, Frances 94, 96, 97, 101, 154
Luro, Horatio 96
Lynch, Frances 141
Lynch, Julia 101
Lynch, Stephen Andrew 73, 101

M

Macfadden-Deauville Amphitheater 119
Manhattan Repertory Theater 119
Marcé, Joaquin Blez 120
Mathews, Edward Nash "Ned" 123, 124
Mathews, Edward Nash, Sr. 122
Mathews, Frances 122
Mathews, Isabel 124
Mathews, James 122
Mathews, Jim (son of James Mathews) 124
McClory, Kevin 149
McEvoy, Freddie 116
McLean, Brownie 28, 106, 107
McLean, Jock 104, 107
Mehle, Aileen 131
Mersman, Marguerite "Mano" 80, 81
Mersman, Otto 80
Mersman, Scudder 80

Miami 36, 42, 49, 53, 60, 76, 83, 85, 89, 109, 110, 112, 115, 119, 129, 139, 142, 149
Miami Art League 127
Miami Beach Bayshore Company 74
Miami Beach Casino 119
Miami Beach Improvement Company 34
Miami Beach News Bureau 68
Miami Beach Public Library and Art Center 120
Miami Beach Symphony Society 119
Miami Beach Yacht Club 39
Miami Herald 21, 139
Miami News 131, 138
Miami Playhouse 119
Miami Woman's Club 120
Million Dollar Pier 81, 85
Minsky's 85, 138
Montgomery Botanical Center 129
Montgomery, Colonel Robert H. 128
Montgomery, Nell 128, 129
Moore, Edward S. 99
Mother Kelly's 109
motorboat racing 39
Munn, Charles Alexander 68, 70, 71
Munn, Frances Drexel 68
Munn, Mary 68

N

Nassau, Bahamas 97, 98, 113, 115, 116, 143, 147
Nautilus Hotel 21, 34, 40, 42, 47, 55, 84, 134
naval air station (NAS) at Opa-Locka 76
New York City 13, 15, 16, 36, 50, 97, 101, 124, 131, 132, 134, 138, 145
Noble, Dana Gibson 93
North Bay Road 59, 84, 96, 131
Northern Dancer 96

Index

O

Oakes, Sir Harry 116
Oceanside Theater 81
Offutt, Emily Battelle 24
Old Forge 140
O'Neill, Joan Gentry Shelden 28, 88, 101, 108, 154
Opa-Locka 76
Orange Bowl Parade 90
Ortiz-Patiño, Jaime 106
Overtown 109

P

Palfrey, Sarah 118
Palm Beach 16, 20, 24, 26, 34, 36, 38, 40, 42, 43, 58, 64, 65, 68, 98, 99, 104, 107, 115, 116, 119, 124, 127, 147, 150, 152, 153
Palmer, Attorney General A. Mitchell 140
Palmer, Peggy 140
Palm Island 134
Palm Island Latin Quarter 58, 108
Pan American Seaplane Base, at Dinner Key 85
Pancoast Hotel 55
Pancoast, Russell 26, 120
Pancoast, Thomas Jessup 16, 23, 34, 119
Paris, France 134, 136
Parrot Jungle 60, 64
parties and balls 30, 33, 34, 45, 96, 130, 131, 136, 138, 145
Patio Bruno 139
Patterson, Lawrence 122
Pawley, William "Bill" 35, 76, 77, 79
Pepper, Representative/Senator Claude 129
Peterson, Jane 127
Philadelphia, Pennsylvania 24, 26, 33, 49, 65, 128, 138
Phillips, J. Marquette 140
Pinetree Drive 145
Putnam, Cleveland 35, 131

Q

Quarterdeck Club 36, 39

R

Rasmussen, Clarice 111
Rentschler, B. Joan. *See* Sawyer, Joan
restricted club membership 24, 150, 154
Reynolds, Marianne O'Brien 102, 103
Reynolds, Patrick 102, 103
Reynolds, Richard Joshua "Dick" 77, 102
Reynolds, Richard S., Jr. 101
Reynolds, Virginia Sargeant 101
Rich, Helen 34
Riggs, Bobby 42
Ritz-Carlton Garden, New York City 139
RKO 94
Robertson, Edwin 122
Romfh, Edward 36
Romfh, Jules 36, 45
Romfh, Lawrence 45
Roney, Newt 122
Roney Plaza 36, 42, 50, 55, 101, 122, 127
Royal Palm Club 109, 110
Rubirosa, Porfirio 103, 104, 106
Runyon, Damon 68, 109
Russell, John 74

S

Sailer, Marion Crozer 50, 52
Sanchez, Jorge 113
Sanchez, Julio 113
Sarazen, Gene 35
Sawyer, Joan 132, 133, 134, 136
Saxony Hotel 81
Scherbatoff, Prince Georges Alexandrovich Stroganoff 42
Schrafft, Brownie. *See* McLean, Brownie
Schrafft, George 28, 107
Scott, Valerie 141
Seller, Earnie 90
Seminole tribe 46, 71

INDEX

Shelden, Charles "Chuck" 108
Sigrist, Beatrice 147, 149
Sigrist, Frederick 147
Sigrist, Fredericka 147, 149
Simmons, Bessie 130
Simmons, John George 130
Sinatra, Frank 152
Slattery's Hurricane 74, 76
Smathers, Frank, Jr. 140
Smathers, Representative/Senator George A. 140
Smith, Nevada 138
Smits, Larry 68, 139
Snedigar, Mayor Louis F. 119
Soames, Mary 64
Sopwith, Sir Thomas 147
Spencer-Churchill, John George Vanderbilt Henry 64
Spicer-Simson, Margaret Schmidt 125
Spicer-Simson, Theodore 124, 125
Spring Lake, New Jersey 19, 42, 138
Springtime for Henry 81, 82
Staley, Augustus E. 53
Star Island 77, 79
Stevens, Marti 54
Stevers, Belle 81, 82, 125
Stevers, Richard 81, 82
Stewart, Janet Rhinelander 68
Stewart, William Rhinelander 68
Stiglich (Capasso), Lucille 144, 145
Stiltsville 36
Sulgrave Club, Washington, D.C. 140
Sulzberger, Arthur Hays 94
Sunny Isles Club 111
Sunset Island Company 74
Sunset Islands 53, 73, 74, 101, 122, 134
Surf Club 24, 28, 30, 36, 40, 45, 58, 61, 68, 74, 88, 96, 101, 108, 121, 127, 129, 131, 136, 139, 147
Surfside 24, 31, 111, 151
Sweny, Robert 104

T

Tahiti 80
Talbert, Billy 138
Talbott, Harold Elstner 71
Talbott, Margaret "Peggy" Thayer 70
Tanton, Lee 134
Taylor, Elizabeth 77, 79
Taylor, Sara Sothern 79
tennis 26, 36, 40, 42, 45, 99, 118
Topping, Daniel 95, 104, 108
Truman, President Harry S. 117
Tully, William J. "Bill" 40, 42
Twentieth Century Fox 74

U

University of Miami 26, 30, 61, 90, 125

V

Valentino, Rudolph 132
Vanderbilt, Consuelo, Duchess of Marlborough 64
Vanderbilt, Rosamund Lancaster Warburton 99
Vanderbilt, William Kissam, II 85, 99
Vandercar, Lewis 127
Venetian Causeway 15, 50, 152
Venetian Islands 83
Versailles (hotel) 55, 57, 98
Villa Tranquilla 74
Villa Vizcaya. *See* Vizcaya Museum and Gardens
Vizcaya Museum and Gardens 127, 129
von Poushental, Baroness Kuhn (Adele) 129
von Poushental, Baron Vladimir Kuhn 129

W

Walters, Lou 108
Warburton, Rosemary. *See* Chisholm, Rosemary Warburton Gaynor
Warden, Archibald Adam 42

Index

Washington Art Gallery 123, 124, 125, 127
Washington Avenue 122
Washington, D.C. 33, 64, 140
Washington Post 107
Washington Storage Company 122
Webster, Harold Tucker "Webby" 38
Westervelt, Effie 153
Westervelt, George Conrad 153
Westervelt, Rieta Brabham Langhorne 153, 154
WGBS 53
Whiting, Frank B. 118
Widener, Gertrude 65
Widener, Joseph E. 52, 65, 71
Widener, Peter Arrell Browne, II 65
Widmark, Richard 74, 76
Windsor, Duke and Duchess of 115, 147
WKAT 53
Wofford, Tatem, Jr. 131
Wolfsonian-Florida International University 123
Wolfson, Mitchell "Micky" 123
Wood, Garfield "Gar" 16, 24, 99, 141, 143, 144, 146
Woolworth, Norman Bailey 117
World War I 140
World War II 58, 76, 93, 99
Worth Avenue Gallery 124
Wrightsman, Charles 70, 117
Wrightsman, Irene 117

Y

yachting 16, 36, 39, 96, 113, 115, 116, 118
Young, Howard 77

ABOUT THE AUTHOR

Deborah C. Pollack graduated with honors from Temple University with a degree in art history. As Deborah Courtney, she performed in numerous television commercials and for three years starred on the soap opera *Love of Life*. She then became a fine art dealer and eventually, revisiting her background in art history, an author. Her books include *Visual Art and the Urban Evolution of the New South* (with "Miami, Miami Beach, and Coral Gables" as one of the chapters); *Palm Beach Visual Arts*; *Felix De Crano: Forgotten Artist of the Flagler Colony*; *Bad Scarlett: The Extraordinary Life of the Notorious Southern Beauty Marie Boozer* (selected for display at a women's historical conference); and *Laura Woodward: The Artist Behind the Innovator Who Developed Palm Beach*, which won an award from Florida Memorial University for making "a significant contribution to advancing the awareness of women's history." Pollack's essays are in the *New Encyclopedia of Southern Culture* and *Central to Their Lives: Women Artists in the Johnson Collection*. Articles have appeared in such periodicals as the *American Art Review*, *Tequesta* (the scholarly journal of HistoryMiami), *Antiques and Art Around Florida*, *New York History Review* and *The Tustenegee* (the Historical Society of Palm Beach County journal). She lives with her husband, Edward, in Palm Beach, Florida, where they own Edward and Deborah Pollack Fine Art.

Visit us at
www.historypress.com